MODERN
NATIONS
—OF THE
WORLD

JORDAN

BY KAREN WILLS

LUCENT BOOKS
P.O. BOX 289011
SAN DIEGO, CA 92198-9011

TITLES IN THE MODERN NATIONS OF THE WORLD SERIES INCLUDE:

Austria
Brazil
Canada
China
Cuba
Egypt
England
Ethiopia
Germany
Greece
Haiti
India
Ireland
Italy
Japan
Jordan

Kenya
Mexico
Norway
Poland
Russia
Saudi Arabia
Scotland
Somalia
South Africa
South Korea
Spain
Sweden
Switzerland
Taiwan
The United States
Vietnam

On Cover: Amman City, Jordan

Library of Congress Cataloging-in-Publication Data

Wills, Karen.
    Jordan / by Karen Wills.
        p.   cm. — (Modern nations of the world)
Includes bibliographical references and index.
    ISBN 1-56006-822-1 (lib. bdg. : alk. paper)
    1. Jordan—Juvenile literature.   [1. Jordan.]   I. Title.   II. Series.
    DS153.W53   2001
    956.95—dc21

                                                00–010096

Copyright © 2001 by Lucent Books, Inc.
P.O. Box 289011, San Diego, CA 92198-9011
Printed in the U.S.A.

CONTENTS

INTRODUCTION

JORDAN: THE MIDDLE OF THE MIDDLE EAST

The kingdom of Jordan is located in the geographic middle of the historically and politically turbulent Middle East. This centrality has created special opportunities and special challenges for its people. Steeped in Arab tradition, Jordanians cherish ancient values of honor, courage, and generosity. They also treasure a rich culture of Arabic language, music, and visual arts. However, they inhabit a resource-poor region that limits their ability to survive the harsh demands of both nature and human conflict.

Geography has been both kind and cruel to Jordan. With a semiarid to arid climate, it is mostly desert. Although poor in natural resources, it is positioned on a geographically strategic land bridge that connects North Africa with Europe, Asia Minor, Mesopotamia, and portions of the Far East. Its western region includes the Jordan River Valley, a source of precious freshwater vital to agriculture and to life in a desert region. In the south, the port of Aqaba provides access to the Red Sea.

Jordan has therefore provided conquering armies, trade caravans, and migratory peoples with a corridor that avoids passage through deserts where only the self-reliant Bedouin nomads could survive. Historically, ambitious world powers recognized Jordan's strategic value; Jordan has thus been host to profitable merchant caravans and, less happily, to passing conquerors.

The history of Jordan has created many vivid images. In biblical terms, these include Abraham, patriarch of the Old Testament, gazing on the thriving lands to which God had directed him, or Jesus being baptized in the waters of the Jordan River. In political and religious terms, Jordan witnessed ancient Greek and Roman conquerors and Arab forces sweeping north to spread the faith of Islam. Medieval crusaders reestablished Christianity in the Holy Land only to be displaced by the Islamic Ottoman Turks. The Arab Revolt of

World War I raises romantic images of Bedouin warriors pounding across desert sands on their camels to fight for long-awaited independence.

Contemporary Jordan produced King Hussein, a courageous, practical, moderate leader who balanced the demands of the Arab world and the reality of a Jewish state in its midst. Jordan has gained and lost the West Bank of the Jordan River in military and political struggles. It has assimilated hundreds of thousands of displaced Palestinian

The Jordan River provides precious fresh water for a country that is mostly desert.

Jordan's current leader, King Abdullah bin al-Hussein, assumed constitutional powers in February 1999.

refugees, and it has coped with the pressure of international debt.

Jordan's current leader is a young, reform-minded monarch who encourages democratization, free enterprise in a growing economy, and environmental awareness. Jordan is moving into the twenty-first century aware of its own importance as a seasoned leader in the Arab world. Jordanians look forward to the future as well as back to their rich heritage, hopeful that they may continue on the path to prosperity and peace.

GEOGRAPHY AND EARLY HISTORY

Jordan's geographic position—in the middle of the Middle East, bordering two vital waterways—has significantly shaped its political history. It borders Syria, Iraq, and Saudi Arabia, and has the longest border (one hundred forty-eight miles) with Israel of any Arab country. Israel lies to the west, as does the mainly Israeli-occupied West Bank (so named because it is on the west side of the Jordan River). Most of Jordan's borders are arbitrarily drawn rather than following natural phenomena such as mountain ranges, rivers, or coasts. Jordan's land area is 37,738 square miles, which includes a sixteen-mile coastline at the Gulf of Aqaba on the Red Sea at Jordan's southern tip.

Topographically, Jordan can be divided into three main regions: the Jordan River Valley, the highlands, and the desert. The fertile Jordan River Valley runs north to south from Syria along the border with Israel to the Dead Sea. The River ends there. The Jordan valley continues south as desert to the Gulf of Aqaba.

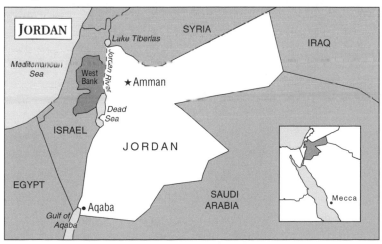

The Jordanian highlands, a narrow strip of territory where most of the population lives, parallel the river valley. The rest of the country, 82 percent, is desert. The desert, a region of scattered oases, extremely hot temperatures, and scant rain, supports little life.

In ancient times, the territories that make up present-day Jordan were crisscrossed by many migrating peoples. The Jewish patriarch Abraham, or Abram, was the first leader known by name to cross the Jordan River and enter the Jordan River Valley, referred to as the land of Canaan in the Old Testament of the Bible. According to Middle East scholar and author Robert St. John, when Abraham first saw the river valley some four thousand years ago, it was an

> ancient place, for man had lived here already for thousands of years. There were sizable cities, more of them on the east side of the river because on that side there were more abundant sources of water. In whatever direction Abram looked he saw thriving and populous villages.[1]

Abraham and his tribe were just one of many small groups displaced from their homelands by war who wandered through the Jordan Valley seeking a new place to live. In this desert region, water was vitally important, and always, the presence of water beckoned the travelers. An old Arab proverb says "It is the duty of each man in his lifetime to beget a son, plant a tree and dig a well."[2]

Thus the Jordan River, a 190-mile stretch of freshwater that might seem unimportant in more water-blessed lands, has been and remains a priceless resource in Jordan, a country that today is four/fifths desert. The river's source is Syria's Mount Herman; its main tributaries are the Yarmouk River, which forms part of the border between Jordan and Syria, and the Nahr as-Zarqa, which flows north of Jordan's capital city, Amman. With precipitous waterfalls the Jordan flows south into the north end of Lake Tiberius, also known as the Sea of Galilee, in Israel. At the lake's southern end, the river passes into the beginning of the Jordan River Valley.

The Jordan has cut a deep bed in a geologic fault known as the Rift Valley. The river does not run straight, but meanders through that depression until it pours into the Dead Sea. From biblical times until the fourteenth century, thickets covering

the twists and turns of the river's banks were home to lions, tigers, and wild boars. However, beyond its banks, then as now, thanks to the fresh waters of the Jordan, agriculture could thrive. The Jordan ends as its waters flow into the Dead Sea.

From the early Bronze Age (3150–2200 B.C.) on, inhabitants of the Valley of the Jordan, the cities of the plain (five cities including Sodom and Gomorrah, situated near the Dead Sea), and the Wadi al-Araba, (the depression of the Rift Valley as it continues south from the Dead Sea to the Gulf of Aqaba on the Red Sea) lived near important trade routes. These routes were essential links to the East for Mediterranean peoples. Ships bearing gems, spices, and silks from China and India sailed the Indian Ocean to harbors on the Red Sea. From seaports such as Aqaba their cargoes were reloaded onto camel caravans for transport north.

Such caravans became a common sight in Jordanian territories. Their stopping places became centers of commerce, bazaars where villagers and Bedouin (nomadic Arabs) could trade camels and wares for goods from the traveling merchants. Some of these centers, such as Beth Shan, became prosperous cities.

Salt-crusted rocks along the Dead Sea.

THE DEAD SEA

At thirteen hundred feet below sea level, the Dead Sea is the lowest place on earth. It is six miles long and varies from three to ten miles wide. Its depth is at most 1,310 feet. The total area covered by water is 405 miles.

Besides being notable for its low surface, the Dead Sea is significant for its chemical composition. It is about four times saltier than the Atlantic Ocean. The Dead Sea's chemical content makes a gallon of its water weigh 12.25 pounds compared with an ordinary gallon of water at 8.33 pounds. Such density also makes it easy for a swimmer to float effortlessly in the Dead Sea and supports the myth that it is impossible to drown in its waters.

Chemicals in the water include potash, potassium, bromine, magnesium, chlorine, and sulfur. Bitumin, an oily substance sometimes called pitch, floats in chunks in the water. The Egyptians used bitumin for mummification. Romans used it in their medicines. Historically, people living along the shores of the Dead Sea collected bitumin for commercial purposes. Flammable bitumin may have played a role in the burning of Sodom and Gomorrah, two of the cities of the plain referred to in the Bible and believed to have been situated on the shores of the Dead Sea. Flames from burning chunks of bitumin in the lake may have reached buildings on shore, contributing to the fiery destruction.

Many caravans followed a route reaching from the city of Amman in the north, south to the Gulf of Aqaba. This was the King's Highway, or the Way of Kings, which paralleled the Jordan River to the east. It served as an important link in the international route connecting Cairo to Babylon and brought the people of the Jordan River Valley in contact with the outside world. The people of the valley, no longer isolated, could learn from, and share their own knowledge with, the rest of the world through contact with traders from such places as Egypt, Mesopotamia, Anatolia, and Cyprus.

EARLY INVASIONS

The caravan and military routes of Jordanian lands made the region an inviting and convenient destination for people seeking power and commercial opportunities. For example, in about 1750 B.C. the warlike Hyksos, possibly an element

of the many adventurers and soldiers of fortune who fre-
quented the Middle East at the time, conquered the northern
regions of Jordanian lands and, ultimately, Egypt, which they
controlled for 150 years.

The Hyksos ushered in a new kind of warfare. They wore
armor and rode to battle in chariots. They introduced their
new military techniques and culture to the valley, including
the strategy of building fortifications to protect key cities, as
well as the custom of creating burial grounds outside a city
to separate the population from its dead.

The Jordan Valley prospered during the era of Hyksos oc-
cupation. Caravans continued to flow through the region ex-
changing goods between Asia and Africa. Luxury goods from
Egypt became available to people in the Jordan River Valley.

The valley would, however, be the scene of many battles,
one of which lasted three years, when Egypt rose up against
the Hyksos conquerers, forcing them back north. Some Hyksos stayed in the valley as refugees, adding another compo-
nent to the valley's population of Jews and Arabs.

About 1000 B.C., the Jewish king David's military conquests
led to the establishment of his kingdom in Jerusalem and vast
holdings in the region. His son, Solomon, would increase the
family riches through acquisition of important seaports such
as Aqaba.

Khalijal Al-'Aquabah, in Arabic, or the Gulf of Aqaba, is the
northeastern arm of the Red Sea. Of the four countries
touched by the Gulf—Egypt, Israel, Saudi Arabia, and Jordan—only Egypt has a sheltered harbor. But Jordan always
had ports there and the seaport of Aqaba was founded as a
center for economic activity where trading ships could load
and unload cargo.

Solomon married the daughter of an Egyptian pharaoh and
thereby gained possession of trading ports at the Gulf of Aqaba.
When Solomon added such ports to his holdings, and when he
inherited David's lands upon that monarch's death, for the first
time Jordanian lands became part of one vast kingdom.

Because his holdings were so extensive, Solomon had no
interest in acquiring more territory through military aggression, but instead wished to keep what he already possessed
by ruling it wisely. Solomon ruled his kingdom in an orderly
and productive way for forty years during which the people of
the Jordan River Valley lived in peaceful prosperity, resenting

Solomon's marriage to an Egyptian princess added the trading ports of the Gulf of Aqaba to Jordan's kingdom.

only Solomon's heavy taxation to support his defense forces and his military draft to supply soldiers for his great army. However, in general, life in Jordanian territories was good. For example, great brass founderies constructed in the valley near the Dead Sea attracted many workers to the area, contributing to its prosperity.

However, upon Solomon's death, the Jordanian region became a pawn on the chessboard of rival empires. From the north, the Assyrian empire achieved control of the area from 841 B.C. until 612 B.C.

Eastern empires raided the territory until the Babylonians conquered it in 587 B.C. The Babylonians killed many, and as a result, according to scholar Robert St. John,

> in the Valley the total population decreased, some towns and villages were abandoned, and a tendency developed among the people on both banks to live in strongly fortified cities whenever possible. There was even a decline in the expertness with which the Valley people tilled their soil.[3]

In 538 B.C. the Persians, under Cyrus the Great, conquered the Babylonians. However, the Persian reign would not last long.

GREEKS AND ROMANS

In 332 B.C., Alexander the Great led his Greek armies across Jordan from Macedonia after he defeated the Persians. Intent on reaching Egypt, he left the Jordanian lands relatively unmolested. However, his army's presence as an occupying force was enough to introduce Greek culture, with its dynamic interest in philosophy, literature, and the arts, to the region. Under Greek rule, Jordanian territories experienced a period of prosperity that brought new building projects, new cities, and an increase in trade. Greek garrisons, or forts, were scattered through the valley and Greek colonists arrived. Greek shrines appeared and some valley dwellers began to worship Greek gods. Valley dwellers adopted Greek fashions and included Greek slang in their conversations. Debates and dialogues in the style of the Greeks became part of the lives of people of the valley.

Main street of Jerash, a Greek and Roman trading town during 1st–3rd centuries.

After Alexander's death the area of present-day Jordan became part of the Greek Empire allotted to one of his generals, who would become Ptolemy I, pharaoh of Egypt. Another general, Seleucid, challenged Ptolemy and fighting ensued in the region until Seleucid prevailed in 198 B.C.

However, the Greeks fell to the army of the Roman general Pompey, who took Damascus (now in Syria) in 64 B.C. and Jerusalem in 63 B.C. The Romans installed Herod as king of the region. During Herod's reign, the Jews of the region, oppressed by their Roman conquerers, became increasingly vocal in their dissatisfaction. One orator and preacher whom the Romans saw as a particular troublemaker was Jesus.

The life of Jesus inspired the rise of Christianity. In his life, Jesus, thought by Christians to be the Son of God, traversed the region. He is believed to have been baptized in the Jordan River and to have taught on its banks.

The Jews' political dissension became an open revolt against Rome in A.D. 66. Rome retaliated by sending the Jews into exile, the first step on the path that would lead, ultimately, to their return and the establishment of the State of Israel in 1948. The scattering of the Jews, known as the Diaspora, might be considered the source of much of the turmoil that exists in Jordan and the rest of the Middle East today.

The Roman Empire alternately tolerated and persecuted Christianity until A.D. 313, when Emperor Constantine legalized the religion, and it became the accepted faith of the empire. The Arabs of Jordanian territories, exposed through trade and invasions to the outside world's advanced societies, had by now became familiar with different religions. They began to be interested in spiritual teachings that went beyond their own paganism.

Christians believe Jesus was baptized in the Jordan River and that he taught along its banks.

Christianity seemed to answer the spiritual needs of some of the people of the region. Christian shrines, monuments, and at least twenty churches, some headed by powerful bishops, appeared east of the Jordan River in the territory of the Eastern Roman, or Byzantine, Empire. Christian schools were estab-

lished, and Christian pilgrims from around the Roman Empire came to visit the Christian holy sites such as the place of Jesus' baptism, thus reinforcing the region's focus on Christianity.

NABATAEANS

While the Persians, Greeks, and Romans successively invaded and conquered Jordanian territories in the north, one Arab people, the Nabataeans, managed to remain free in the southern region for generations. Originally tent-dwelling nomads of Saudi Arabia, they eventually settled about fifty miles south of the Dead Sea, where they carved a stronghold, the city of Petra, from rose-red stone. Monasteries, temples, and tombs were all shaped from rock.

As the Nabataeans turned from plundering passing caravans to becoming traders themselves, Petra became one of the great centers of commerce of the Middle East. The Nabataeans dominated the important silk and spice trade from India and China because they built trade roads guarded by evenly spaced forts. By this means they provided military protection to their caravans.

The Nabataeans carved the city of Petra entirely out of rock.

One of the reasons Petra held so long against the Roman army is that there is only one main entry to the city, a gorge, the sik, about a mile in length, and difficult to find. The Romans overcame the Nabataeans only by discovering the source of water to Petra and damming it. After subduing them, however, the Romans allowed the Nabataeans much freedom as they served as a buffer kingdom against desert tribes. The Nabataeans operated from Syria to the Arabian Peninsula from the fifth century until the trade routes altered in the seventh century.

Because they were originally nomads, the Nabataeans had intimate knowledge of the desert. They were an inventive people who made lasting contributions to human survival in

WADI RUM

Eighty-two percent of Jordan is desert that lies east of the Jordanian highlands. The northern desert is composed of hardened lava and basalt, the southern part of sandstone and granite, sand dunes, and salt flats. Oases (fertile spots in the desert where water is found) and wadis (rocky declivities which are dry except in the rainy season) dot both north and south.

The most famous desert region is Wadi Rum, a valley located northeast of Aqaba close to the Desert Highway. Towering rock formations known as jebels have been carved there by hot desert winds.

Rock art from ancient peoples can still be seen in the village of Rum. The Nabataeans once built a temple there, and its ruins remain as well. Today, Wadi Rum's human residents number about four thousand villagers and Bedouin nomads. The only structures are Bedouin tents, concrete houses and shops, and the Desert Patrol Corps fort headquarters.

Wadi Rum is also home to a vast variety of wildlife. Bird species abound, from the small Sinai rosefinch to the great thermals such as the white Egyptian vulture and the griffin vulture. Mammals include the fox, hyena, desert hare, ibex, hedgehog, and gerbil, as well as the little hyrax, in appearance somewhat like a rabbit, whose hooflike claws enable it to climb the rock crevasses it inhabits. The poisonous Palestine viper shares the region with numbers of butterflies.

Wadi Rum has a rich human and natural history. Most of all it is the embodiment of the spectacular, boundless romance of the desert.

A Bedouin camp at the base of a spectacular jebel.

that arid climate. For example, they developed a system of irrigation near the Jordan River that was rediscovered and imitated in the twentieth century. They were skilled in the collection and storage of water. Their engineers developed ways to store nearly all available water, from scarce rain to torrential flash floods. Their methods minimized evaporation and some of their cisterns and reservoirs, unearthed by archaeologists, have now been restored to use in modern times.

The Nabataeans also developed a system of terracing to control erosion. This led to their marked success in agriculture, bringing productivity to levels previously unknown in the Jordanian territories.

THE MUSLIM CONQUEST

Until the seventh century, the Arabs of the Jordanian territories, conquered by different empires, continued to live, fight, and worship in separate tribal groups, a mixture of pagan and Christian societies. Then, a great religious movement united these groups in Islam, a faith that followed the teachings of the prophet Muhammad (570–632). Islam called for submission to the will of God, with no separation between religious and state authority. It therefore led to centralized political power. The individual, community, and society in general were subject to the rule of descendants of Muhammad, known as imams, or caliphs, who inherited positions of power.

Born in Mecca, in Saudi Arabia, Muhammad communicated a message that inspired devoted Arab armies known as the Sword of Islam to sweep from Arabia, conquering the Byzantines first in the bordering region of Jordan, and then in more distant countries. The forces of Islam struggled to control both the religious practices and the profitable trade routes of the conquered regions.

In the seventh century, the caliph Muawrayhah moved the Islamic capital from Mecca to Damascus in Syria. Jordan thrived during this time, as desert-loving caliphs made nearby Jordan a resort area where they built elegant castles and hunting lodges.

To the followers of Islam, called Muslims, pilgrimage to Mecca became an important religious duty. Each Muslim is to make the pilgrimage during his or her lifetime because Mecca is the birthplace of the Prophet. The route from Damascus followed the East Bank to the city of Ma'an in Jordanian territories before turning toward Mecca. Tribes in control of the area found both trade caravans and pilgrims a welcome source of income when they charged them protection money to pass safely on their way.

The prosperous times ended for the Jordanian region when a Sunni group known as the Abbasids moved the Muslim capital to Baghdad in 762. (Sunnis are a large, orthodox division of Islam.) For two and a half centuries Jordan languished as a backwater. As the Abbasids weakened over time, Bedouin Arabs took back control of various areas in the Jordanian territory.

Whether in times of affluence or economic stagnation, the Islamic Arabs influenced the culture of Jordanians more than any other controlling power. The search for knowledge was a sacred idea to the Muslims. They sought spiritual awareness and understanding. They wished not only to learn all they could regarding their sacred book, the Koran, but also to hone the practical skills necessary to apply its tenets for the good of society.

An encampment of Muslims on pilgrimage to Mecca. Muslims consider the pilgrimage an important religious duty.

The Muslims introduced new concepts of religion through the teachings of the Prophet and the Koran. They built on earlier work of Greeks, Iranians, and Indians to make great contributions in science and mathematics, including the introduction of the zero in figuring equations and the development of trigonometry and algebra. The Muslims believed the search for truth in philosophy was a noble human endeavor and they translated the work of many of the Greeks such as Aristotle and Plato into Arabic. They followed the Greeks in their pursuit of truth through reason, logic, and the laws of nature. In medicine, they were first to diagnose smallpox and measles, and developed the use of animal gut for sutures.

THE CRUSADES

Islamic power in the Middle East would not go unchallenged. The challenge, which came from the Christian Europeans, focused on the city of Jerusalem. Jerusalem was and is a city sacred to three great world religions. It is where the Jewish king Solomon built a great temple; it is the site of many events related to the life of Jesus; and it contains the Dome of the Rock, the place from which, according to Islamic belief, the Prophet ascended into heaven.

In 1097, in far-off Cleremont, France, Pope Urban II called for a papal army to retake Jerusalem, the City of the Holy Sepulchre (the sacred place of Jesus' tomb), from the Muslims. Thus, the Crusades, a series of military expeditions and holy wars, were born.

Europeans joined the Crusades for varied reasons. Some went from a devoutly religious desire to restore Christianity to the region. Christian churches were being destroyed and Christian pilgrims routinely victimized by a sort of robber industry that had become established along the routes where Christians traveled to such places as the site of Jesus' baptism and the Dead Sea. Some crusaders went because they hungered for profit. Many young squires and nobles went in search of free lands to be seized as spoils of war when they successfully conquered the Muslims, while others just craved adventure.

The crusaders stormed Jerusalem in 1099. Following their army's victory, many soldiers continued east to the Jordan River Valley. Some wished to be baptized in the Jordan River, but others went to fell trees to build the army's defense fortifications.

After the fall of Jerusalem, the valley of the Jordan hosted crowds of European tourists and pilgrims. Most of these visitors, as well as the crusaders, chose to return home, but some stayed and established feudal rule over the people. Each lord built a castle on some high place. Villages under the lord's domination had to support him through payment of a variety of stiff taxes. In exchange for the lord's protection, villagers could be drafted to serve in his private army if local quarrels broke out.

The feudal lords lived privileged lives. Because their castles were situated along trade routes, caravans arrived from the East with silks, perfumes, jewels, spices, and brocades. These new valley aristocrats entertained lavishly and pursued leisure activities such as hunting and falconry. Theirs was a good life and they meant to stay.

SALADIN

Conflict between Muslims and Christian victors of the First Crusade over possession of the Holy Land would continue for a century. A brilliant military leader, Yusuf ibn-Ayyub Salah-ed-Din, called Saladin by the crusaders, arose from the Muslim military officer ranks. In 1174, Saladin deposed the caliph under whom he served as grand vizier and seized control as sultan of Egypt and Syria. He successfully challenged the crusaders by attacking their fortresses. After one crusader broke a truce with him, Saladin declared a jihad, or holy war, against all Christians in the Holy Land.

Saladin's army gradually took land back from the crusaders, culminating in the seizure of Jerusalem in 1187. Though there would be other Crusades, the European invaders never again reached the Jordan Valley. Christian pilgrims were permitted to peaceably visit Jerusalem and the Jordan River only after Saladin and King Richard the Lion-Hearted of England, a leader of the Third Crusade, signed a truce in 1192.

Saladin was renowned as a scholar and just leader. During his reign he restored unity, broken during the post-Crusade years of European dominance, to the Arab world. He gained the respect of Westerners and Easterners alike.

MONGOLS AND MAMELUKES

During Saladin's time, Muslims, as well as hundreds of thousands of Jews under his rule, lived in general prosperity. However, the 1200s brought hardship to the Jordan Valley. The Mongols swept down from China, through Jordanian territory, heading for the Mediterranean and the Red Sea. The Mongol hordes murdered, pillaged, plundered, and destroyed churches, mosques, and synagogues wherever they went. The valley suffered particularly from the Mongol destruction of precious irrigation systems.

But a new element in the valley, the Mamelukes, a military force of former Egyptian slaves, defeated the Mongols in 1260 at the battle of Ain Jalut near the Jordan River. The Mamelukes were able soldiers but inept administrators. Failing to achieve lasting stability, they ruled the region for 267 years with a total of 47 leaders. Mameluke sultans were selected from senior commanders, but rivalries for leadership often became bloody, and most Mameluke sultans died at the hands of assassins.

The Mamelukes fought off a Mongolian invasion in 1260, and drove the last of the crusaders from the Middle East in

Shobeq was one of the many crusader fortresses which fell to Saladin's army.

1291. However, Jordanian territories fared poorly during this period. The Mamelukes subjected the people to heavy taxation and a devastating plague, known as the Black Death, spread from Egypt through the Middle East and eventually to Europe. The plague not only decimated the population but left weakened survivors without the skills and manpower required to service roads and cities.

THE OTTOMAN TURKS

The Ottoman Turks, invaders from Central Asia, ended Mameluke rule when they annexed Syria, Jordan, and Palestine in 1516. At first the Ottoman Empire's rule furthered commercial and intellectual pursuits in the Jordan River Valley. In 1520 the sultan Suleiman the Magnificent ordered the walls of the holy city of Jerusalem to be rebuilt, which raised his popularity with the populace. However, over the next two centuries, corruption slowly eroded the Ottoman regime. Neglected, Jordanian territories stagnated.

By the eighteenth century, the Ottomans, in serious decline, were putting little effort into improving Jordanian territories. They taxed their subjects heavily and retained tight control in the cities while allowing rural areas to go unprotected, with farmers left prey to raids by outlaws. In spite of later Ottoman efforts to establish order via military and police garrisons, the Bedouin tribes continued to raid one another, outlying villages, and travelers of all kinds, causing fear and general disruption. Bedouin tribal law prevailed in the desert.

Although rulers and ruled were both Muslim, the Arabs hated the Ottoman officials and military who governed the provinces established by the Ottoman sultan in Cairo, whom they considered foreign oppressors. Bedouin uprisings occurred in 1905 and in 1910. Because Bedouin sheiks posed a threat to peace in the region, the Turks finally resorted to paying the Bedouin chieftains to safeguard Ottoman railways rather than seeing them subjected to Bedouin raids.

Arguably the greatest contribution of the Turks would be the Hijaz Railway. Its purpose was to carry Muslims on their pilgrimages and to achieve strong military control of the Arabian Peninsula. By 1908 its trains ran from Istanbul, Turkey, to Aleppo in Syria, then to Damascus, Amman, and finally to Medina in Saudi Arabia, the second most sacred place in Islam, where the prophet Muhammad is buried.

The railway notwithstanding, four hundred years of Ottoman rule did not foster economic development in the Jordanian territory. According to author Robert St. John,

It is doubtful whether there had ever been, anywhere, a land as sick as the Jordan Valley in the late nineteenth century. . . . As a result of the ravages of war and centuries of . . . neglect, the great cities had crumbled, dikes and dams had been destroyed, canals were clogged and overgrazing [by goats] had left the hills denuded, thus encouraging destructive erosion and a once proud people had sunk into hopeless poverty.[4]

THE HIJAZ RAILROAD

Although the Ottoman Turks did little to develop the Jordanian territories they conquered, they did make one lasting contribution to the infrastructure: the Hijaz Railway. Work started in Ma'an on May 2, 1900, and by 1908 tracks reached from Damascus to Mecca. The Turks' purpose in building the railway was twofold. First, it transported pilgrims to Islamic holy cities, and second, it allowed the Ottoman government to more easily control the sharifs of Mecca. Besides facilitating pilgrimages and Turkish dominance, the Hijaz Railway served as a trade route between Jordan and Syria.

Lawrence of Arabia traveled on the Hijaz Railway and also sabotaged it during the Arab Revolt. Today, tourists can board, and dine in, the same car he rode.

The trains are still powered by the old steam engines or diesel engines and are of historic interest in themselves. They are not fast—the trip from Amman to the Syrian border may take eight hours. However, it is a romantic journey through the vast and beautiful desert landscape, transporting the traveler back to the time of pilgrims on holy journeys and Arabs fighting for their independence.

A railway station of the Hijaz Railroad.

But the situation was not hopeless. Though the Arabs of Jordanian territories were suspicious of Westerners as a result of the Crusades, after experiencing deterioration under Ottoman rule, they began to think contact with other nations might provide opportunities to improve their situation.

The French emperor Napoléon had invaded Egypt in 1798 and his campaign there attracted European interest in the Middle East. European tourists became a familiar sight to Arabs in the nineteenth century. The British, who drove the French out of Egypt in 1801, became a continuing presence in the Middle East after they took control of Egypt in 1882. The British also gained control of the Suez Canal, built by France in 1869, which connected the Mediterranean with the Red Sea and was therefore important economically as an international route for sea trade.

In World War I the British fought the Germans in Europe and the German allies the Turks in the Holy Land, called Palestine. They realized that an Arab rebellion against the Turks might help the British cause. The Arabs were aware of the advantages that might be offered to them from British military technology if they were to form an alliance.

As their desire for independence intensified, urban Arabs and the more remote desert groups began to work separately to weaken the hold of their Ottoman overlords. They found their common leader and spokesman in Hussein ibn Ali al Hashimi, the prince of Mecca and a sharif, or direct descendant of Muhammad. It was this man, Sharif Hussein, who would set in motion the events that would place Jordan on the map as an independent nation.

THE FORMATION OF MODERN JORDAN

The formation of modern Jordan began with the dreams of the man chosen to speak for Arabs who sought independence. As a direct descendant of the prophet Muhammad, Hussein ibn Ali commanded great respect among many Muslims. Even his physical appearance was commanding. Middle East expert and journalist Sandra Mackey writes, "The imperious sharif emitted the aura of authority. His distinguished white beard and white banded turban served as staging for piercing black eyes that paralyzed those who came within his gaze."[5]

Hussein, born in Mecca, had lived with his four sons in Constantinople from 1893 to 1908. There they were well

Sharif Hussein was a direct descendant of the prophet Muhammad.   25

treated, but under involuntary restraint as so-called guests of the caliph who, quite rightly, thought Hussein might cause trouble for the Turks. Nevertheless, in 1908 his request to become religious custodian of Mecca was granted. That holiest city of Islam was located in the Hijaz, the western coastal plains region of what is now Saudi Arabia.

Once there, the fifty-three-year-old Hussein, who besides being descended from the Prophet was head of the Arab Hashemite family, built political power with the tribes of the Hijaz. His position so threatened the Turks that the Turkish governor was sent to depose him. Instead of ousting the sharif, however, the governor found that the only way to avoid a full-scale Arab uprising was to kiss the hem of the sharif's robe in token of respect for the sanctity of his office.

This deference underscored the decline of the Ottoman Empire during the late nineteenth and early twentieth centuries while the Arabs' desire for an independent Arab state grew.

The third political entity to figure in the Middle East of World War I was the British Empire. England was the dominant colonial power in India and Egypt, and was well aware that access to a friendly Hijaz was important to its continued well-being in that region, too. The rich oil fields of the Anglo-Persian Company, for example, located at the head of the Persian Gulf, were a significant British economic interest.

Britain's senior official in Cairo was Lord Horatio Kitchener. In February 1914, Hussein sent his son Abdullah to visit Kitchener and explore the possibility of British support in the event of an open Arab revolt against the Turks. At first the British responded negatively to the overture, but the outbreak of World War I five months later made them reconsider.

In the war, Turkey sided with England's enemy Germany. Britain's main fear for the Middle East was that the Ottoman Empire would call on all Muslims to join in a jihad, or holy war, against the Allied forces of Europe, predominantly Great Britain, France, and Russia, (and, in 1917, the United States).

BRITISH MANEUVERING AND THE ARAB REVOLT

The Arab and British alliance against the Turks progressed through a series of letters. Known as the MacMahon Correspondence, the letters passed between Sir Henry MacMahon, British High Commissioner for Egypt and Sudan, and Hussein. These resulted in an agreement that, with financial support from Britain, the Arabs would fight the Turks. In exchange,

MacMahon promised lands for an Arab state when the Ottomans were defeated. Hussein wrote that the lands under his Sharifian Arab Government should include most of the Arabian Peninsula, Palestine, the land between the eastern shore of the Mediterranean and west of the Jordan River that in biblical times constituted Israel and Judah, Lebanon, Syria (including present day Jordan), and Iraq.

Some historians say MacMahon did not specifically promise Hussein the lands he claimed in the agreement. Others say he was specific enough so that Hussein was justified in believing that a firm agreement existed which included Palestine in the future Arab state. In any event, relying on what he interpreted to be British promises, Hussein committed the Arabs to a revolt against the Ottoman Empire.

King Abdullah approached Lord Horatio Kitchener (pictured) seeking British support for an Arab revolt.

What Hussein did not know was that even as he corresponded with MacMahon, the British, French, and Russians were engaged in secret negotiations to partition the postwar Middle East into zones under their control. Their discussions, known as the Sykes-Picot Agreement, stated that following an Allied victory in the Middle East, control of the territory of Palestine, would be divided between Britain and France. An Arab state would exist in the Arabian Peninsula.

Unaware of Britain's secret dealings, Hussein and his sons launched the Arab revolt on June 5, 1916. On November 2, after Arabs had engaged Turks in a series of skirmishes and battles, Sharif Hussein declared himself king of the Arab lands in a public ceremony at the Great Mosque of Mecca.

As the Arab revolt progressed, the British supplied not only money, arms, and explosives, but military advisers. The most famous of these was T. E. Lawrence, who became known as Lawrence of Arabia. A brilliant and daring military strategist who was already familiar with the Arab world, Lawrence formed a close friendship with Hussein's son Faisal. Their most celebrated exploits involved guerrilla raids that crippled

T. E. Lawrence (seated at right, wearing wristwatch) and Prince Faisal (right of Lawrence) meet with Bedouin sheiks.

the enemy's ability to move troops and supplies. Together, Faisal and Lawrence captured the port of Aqaba and later gathered forces to seize Damascus in October 1918.

While the Arabs were helping win the war in the Middle East, in 1917 the British minister for foreign affairs, Arthur Balfour, and the Zionists engaged in discussions. The Zionist movement arose in the late nineteenth century and called for Jews to immigrate to Palestine, the site of the ancient kingdom of Israel, to reestablish a homeland there. The British hoped such negotiations would gain them international Jewish support for their war effort. As a result of these discussions, the document known as the Balfour Declaration promised British assistance in the creation of the Jewish people's desired home in Palestine.

Arab opposition to the Balfour Declaration was intense, but relaxed somewhat with the open circulation of the text of the document, including the clause "it being clearly understood that nothing should be done which may prejudice the civil and religious rights of existing non-Jewish communities in Palestine."[6]

Thus, the dispute between the Arabs and Jews over control of Palestine, which continues today, was born in the confusion of secret negotiations and private agreements. As author Sandra Mackey explains:

With the flourish of a pen, Palestine became a thrice-promised land. Britain had already pledged Arab independence in the Hussein-MacMahon documents. It then determined Palestine's future as a British colony in the Sykes-Picot Agreement. Now . . . the British embraced the Zionist agenda. Even the British themselves were puzzled.[7]

POSTWAR MANDATES

The process of sorting out the confusion began with the Allied victory. At the end of the war, colonies that had formerly belonged to the defeated Ottoman Empire and Germany were placed under the supervision of politically and technologically developed victor nations. In theory, the supervising nations were to prepare their mandated lands for political

LAWRENCE OF ARABIA

T. E. (Thomas Edward) Lawrence was the key British military officer assisting the Arab Revolt. Born in Wales on August 16, 1888, Lawrence studied archaeology at Oxford, and following graduation worked for a British Museum excavation project in Iraq. At the start of World War I he served in the office of British military intelligence in Cairo.

Then Lawrence met Faisal, Sharif Hussein's third son. They formed a close friendship and fought the Turks together, striking at Turkish rail lines and garrisons in guerrilla raids. Tourists who travel the old route of the Hijaz Railway can still see the remains of derailed coaches—the handiwork of Faisal and Lawrence—protruding from desert sands.

Lawrence's greatest victory came on June 19, 1917, when he and forty men on camels rode eight hundred miles at breakneck speed enlisting Bedouin tribes into an army of one thousand men. With Faisal, they captured the Turkish port of Aqaba on the Red Sea. After the war, Lawrence was included in the British delegation at the Paris Peace conference, where he failed to win support for Arab independence. He returned to England weary and disappointed.

In 1922 Lawrence enlisted in the Royal Air Force under a false name, but was discharged when the press exposed him. With help from prestigious friends, he reenlisted in the Tank Corps as Thomas Edward Shaw and served until 1925. In March 1935 he retired to Clouds Hill, his cottage in Dorset, England. He suffered fatal head injuries from a motorcycle accident two months later.

and economic independence. In practice, the mandated nations were little more than colonies of the more powerful countries who controlled them. Under this system, known as the mandate system, France obtained control of Syria and Lebanon and Britain controlled Palestine.

In 1921, Hussein's son Abdullah threatened to raise an army to drive the French out of Syria. To pacify Abdullah, Winston Churchill, British Secretary of the Colonial Office, subdivided Britain's Palestine mandate along the Jordan River–Gulf of Aqaba line. Abdullah would head the Arab administration as amir of the eastern part, largely a desert expanse, called Transjordan (literally, beyond the Jordan). The British would continue to control Transjordan's finances and foreign policy. Satisfied with this arrangement, Abdullah agreed not to take action against the French.

TRANSJORDAN

The newly established amirite of Transjordan was a small and impoverished country of fewer than four hundred thousand people. About 20 percent of its inhabitants lived in cities; the rest were farmers, villagers, and tribal nomads known as Bedouins. Nearly all of the population, whether settled or nomadic, were Muslim.

One of the first problems Abdullah faced as Transjordan's ruler was confusion in the administration of the new country. Abdullah's treasury consisted mainly of a yearly subsidy provided by the British. To manage treasury appropriations and meet other administrative challenges, the British oversaw the training of an Arab civil service. At the start, according to Jordanian scholar Helen Chapin Metz, "Abdullah ruled directly with a small executive council, much in the manner of a tribal shaykh. British officials handled the problem of defense, finance, and foreign policy, leaving internal political affairs to Abdullah."[8]

Another challenge Abdullah encountered was the question of how to effectively govern a tradition-bound tribal society. The Bedouin, or desert nomads, and some villagers as well, were divided into tribes that relied on their own leaders, rather than state courts, to settle disputes. The Bedouin also feuded with each other, raiding each other's camps and in doing so sometimes ignoring international borders. In addition, the Bedouins were not taxed. That privilege drew resentment from villagers and city dwellers, who paid stiff taxes.

Still, in spite of the problems their behavior caused him, Abdullah believed in the values of a Bedouin society. The desert nomads had a firm commitment to family honor, courage, hospitality to strangers, and self-reliance. Abdullah made it a priority to gain and keep the support of the tribes. He recruited his army from the Bedouin and won their loyalty as a Hashemite king and a descendant of the Prophet.

Even so, when the tradition of tribal raids continued across the newly drawn boundaries of post–World War I Middle Eastern countries and threatened stability in the region, Abdullah decided to act. To suppress the desert outlaws, he asked the British to organize a peacekeeping force among the Arabs. F. G. Peake, a veteran with experience fighting in the territory, combined the Arab police and reserve forces into an effective regular army called the Arab Legion. By 1931 the Arab Legion had made significant strides in enforcing order.

THE DESERT PATROL

Before the existence of Transjordan, the desert Arabs were used to a way of life that included raids against tribes of equal status. They were not at all used to observing international borders in the vast, boundary-less land they inhabited. To police the desert after Palestinian partition, the Desert Patrol, also known as the Camel Corps, or Desert Mobile Force, a 350-member extension of the Arab Legion was created in 1930.

To bring this about, the British transferred Captain John Bagat Glubb who had previously served in Iraq, to the Arab Legion. Glubb spoke Arabic and knew and appreciated Bedouin culture. He had knowledge of the strategies and tactics needed for a desert military unit to operate successfully. He recruited prominent Bedouin men from important tribes and gave them intensive training. These Bedouin were proud of their skills and their close identification with the king. They were successful in patrolling the border and ending border raids.

The Desert Patrol was a 350-member extension of the Arab Legion.

With close cooperation between Abdullah and the British, Transjordan, largely nomadic and tribal, progressed steadily toward both modernization and independence from Britain's control. The British funded improvements in roads, communications, schools, and public services. Nomads were encouraged to cultivate land and attempts were made to provide irrigation for farming. In 1923, Britain recognized Transjordan's status as a national state preparing for independence.

This was what Abdullah wanted. Even as he received much help from Britain, he focused always on autonomy. In 1928 he worked with Britain to create Jordan's first constitution, known as the Organic Law. He established democratic credentials by holding elections for Transjordan's first parliament in 1929. The duty of the resulting Legislative Council was to propose laws that Abdullah, as amir, would pass or veto. He retained the power to issue decrees, and the British retained power to overrule all decisions. In 1934 a new agreement with Britain permitted Abdullah to establish consulates in other Arab countries.

Prince Abdullah officially became king of the new kingdom of Transjordan in May 1946.

In 1939 British power was relaxed and Abdullah restructured the Legislative Council into his own cabinet, the Council of Ministers.

Although aspiring to full independence, Transjordan continued its relationship with Britain during World War II. Transjordan was the only Arab country to give active support to the Allied forces in their fight against the Axis powers of Germany and Italy. Units of the Arab Legion, headed by British officer John Glubb, overthrew a pro-Nazi regime in Iraq and defeated the German-supported Vichy French in Syria. Elements of the legion also guarded British supply lines, pipelines, transportation routes, and installations in Egypt.

Transjordan reaped the rewards of having fought on the winning side when the war ended. A grateful Britain entered into the Anglo-

Transjordanian Treaty of March 22, 1946, which proclaimed Transjordan a kingdom. Abdullah officially became king on May 25, 1946.

POLITICAL MANEUVERING

The fact that the kingdom of Jordan still depended on Britain for substantial monetary aid caused Abdullah problems when he applied for membership in the fledgling United Nations. The Soviet Union vetoed Jordanian membership, claiming that Jordan was still under significant British control. To resolve the issue, Britain agreed in a 1948 treaty to remove all restrictions on Transjordan's self-rule. Britain retained only the right to keep some military and transit bases there, and also pledged to continue financial support for the Arab Legion.

Abdullah's goals did not end with his now-independent kingdom's boundaries. Even during World War II, he, like his father, had continued to dream of a united "Greater Syria" composed of Transjordan, Syria, Palestine, and Iraq. In his vision, this country would be ruled by the Hashemites. Trying to gain support for his dream, he took part in March 1945 in discussions in Cairo that led to formation of the League of Arab States (Arab League). There, he met disappointing opposition to his idea of a Greater Syria.

The Arab League was formed to promote Arab strength and unity. Its founding members were Transjordan, Egypt, Syria, Lebanon, Saudi Arabia, Iraq, and Yemen. The leaders of these Arab countries were alarmed by the growing Zionist movement, which called with increasing intensity for a Jewish homeland to be established in Palestine. From the 1930s on Arabs had increasingly feared displacement, threatened by the influx of thousands of Jews immigrating to Palestine from Europe to escape Nazi persecution. Tensions between the Jews and Arabs increased in the 1940s. Although the war ended, the peace would not last. Arab-Israeli tensions were about to boil over.

BRITISH WITHDRAWAL AND WAR WITH ISRAEL

Tensions between Arabs and Jews made Palestine a major trouble spot for the British Empire by 1947. As a result, Britain asked the United Nations to propose a solution to the problem of Palestine. The United Nations Special Committee on Palestine devised a plan whereby Palestine would be divided into two states, one Arab and one Jewish. Jerusalem would be under international control. The plan met with strong Arab resistance; Abdullah was the only Arab ruler even willing to consider it.

When it became clear that the plan met with too much opposition from others, Britain, hated by the Palestinian Arabs for its friendship with the Zionists, wanted no more of the Palestinian problem. Skirmishes between Palestinians and Israelis had already intensified when Britain relinquished its control of Palestine and withdrew its troops on May 14, 1948. On that same day, in Jerusalem, Jews who had accepted the partition proclaimed the establishment of the independent State of Israel. The Arabs, maintaining their consistent position, rejected what they viewed as a forced partition of their land by the UN plan.

Members of the Arab League, with Abdullah as their commander in chief, attacked Israel one day later. Of the Arab forces, only his Arab Legion was well trained and experienced. They captured a section of Jerusalem, the Old City, which contained principal Muslim holy places as well as the traditional Jewish Quarter, and parts of the West Bank, an area west of the Jordan River and the Dead Sea. Except for Gaza, a strip of land along the Mediterranean seized by Egypt, Israel held all the rest of the mandated territory. The Palestinians, except those who lived in the West Bank region won by Jordan, lost their homeland. Seven hundred thousand people, 60 percent of the Palestinians, became refugees.

THE HASHEMITE KINGDOM OF JORDAN

Arab leaders and delegates from refugee camps in the West Bank voted for union with Jordan, and after a vote of his cabinet and legislature on April 24, 1950, Abdullah formally annexed the West Bank. With the West Bank now officially part of Jordan, its residents, as well as other Palestinians pouring into Jordan as refugees, were granted Jordanian citizenship.

Still, in the international community, only Britain and Pakistan recognized the annexation. Other Arab countries thought Abdullah still harbored ambitions to expand his own Hashemite kingdom. These countries also resented his continuing relationship with the British and suspected him of collusion with Israel, their sworn enemy. In fact, he had negotiated a truce with Israel in 1949.

To add to Abdullah's problems, annexation itself strained Jordan's resources to the breaking point. While the West Bank was an asset as a fertile agricultural center, Jordan was not capable of caring for the sudden increase in its population caused by Palestinian refugees. Before the war, Transjordan's population was about 340,000. Following the war, about 500,000 Palestinian Arabs sought refuge in Transjordan or in the West Bank, which already had 500,000 inhabitants.

PALESTINIAN REFUGEE CAMPS

At first, refugee camps were cities of leaky olive green World War II surplus tents sheltering the Palestinian refugees of the Arab-Israeli War of 1948. The camps were places of grim poverty. Blankets were thin; rations of basic items like flour were meager; water was insufficient; and sanitation facilities were inadequate. The threat of such infectious diseases as dysentery and typhoid was constant. The camps lacked kerosene, so there were no lights after sundown. There were no schools for the children, and no jobs for the men. About half of the refugees had been farmers. They sat outside their tents, frustrated and disoriented without their land. All had to cope with boredom.

Five camps were established: Irbid, Az Azarqa, Ammon New, Al Karamah, and Jabal al Hussein. Most were located near major cities of northwest Transjordan. Over time, the camps grew and were absorbed by the cities themselves. Tents have been replaced by rows of galvanized steel, aluminum, asbestos, or cinderblock structures. Many Palestinians have left the camps and even prospered. Some refuse to leave, vowing to remain until they can return to their homeland, and wanting the world to witness their plight.

The 1967 Six-Day War with Israel brought a new influx of refugees. Six more camps appeared. Refugee camp conditions have improved, however, and today's residents have access to education and health care. The United Nations is a vital source of aid for sustaining Jordan's refugee camp population.

Palestinian refugees at one of Jordan's many refugee camps.

The UN Relief and Works Agency had to provide aid. Even with UN and private help, however, the refugees were a drain on Jordan's food and water supplies.

ASSIMILATING THE PALESTINIANS

Besides straining the resources of Abdullah's kingdom, the Palestinians, now a majority, were not as loyal as the Jordanian Arabs to the Hashemites. Palestinians also tended to be better educated and more sophisticated than the nomadic Bedouins. As the political organization of this new faction grew, the Palestinians pressed for limits to the power of the king and his cabinet, and more control by the people through popular elections.

After the war with Israel, Palestinians had agreed to join Abdullah because they were, after all, homeless. However, they soon came to dislike him. Those with education and professional skills looked down on the Jordanians and on Abdullah as a Bedouin. Devout Muslim Palestinians who lacked skills resented him for his willingness to talk to Israeli leaders. According to journalist Sandra Mackey:

> As for Abdullah, he neither trusted nor particularly respected the Palestinians, yet at the same time, his po-

 ## KING ABDULLAH'S ASSASSINATION

Although many wished him dead, King Abdullah was so intent on linking the West Bank to the East Bank under his rule that he refused to remain safely in Amman. He declined to listen to both American and British ambassadors who warned him that he would be in grave danger of assassination if he went to the huge Al-Aqsa Mosque in Jerusalem. As many as four thousand could worship there at a time, presenting security risks.

On July 20, 1951, wearing a flowing white robe and beige cloak, he arrived with his fifteen-year-old grandson Hussein, who, at his grandfather's request, was in military uniform complete with medals. They removed their shoes at the door of the great mosque. As they crossed the threshold, Mustafa Shukri, a tailor's apprentice and a pro-Nazi sympathizer in a radical Palestinian group, stepped from behind an iron grille. He fired five times, hitting Abdullah in the face and chest. A sixth bullet struck Hussein, but ricocheted off a medal fastened to his uniform.

Terrified worshipers trampled the king's body in their rush to escape. At least twenty bystanders were slain by the king's Arab Legionnaires' firing guns and thrusting bayonets into the panicked crowd.

Abdullah's body was wrapped in a carpet and carried out of the mosque. His friend John Glubb, the British adviser to the Arab Legion, comforted Hussein as they returned to Amman.

litical and territorial interests demanded that he build some base among those who, at the least, disdained him. Drawing some support from privileged Palestinians, Abdullah attempted to erase any sense of separate Palestinian identity within his kingdom. Palestinian history and culture as well as the Palestinian flag were banished from the schools and public forums.[9]

Abdullah's efforts to quell his subjects' dissatisfaction would fail. There had been threats on his life before, and he knew of a plot to kill him, but he refused to stay hidden. On Friday, July 20, 1951, Abdullah traveled to Jerusalem, where an assassin shot and killed him. His body was returned to Amman, where it now rests in the Royal Court.

Abdullah had not fully realized his dreams, but he had brought Jordan to independence and had gained the fertile West Bank. He had begun a careful diplomatic dance to court the Palestinians newly arrived in Jordan while keeping the loyalty of Jordanian Arabs. It would fall to his successor to follow in Abdullah's intricate steps.

3

THE MODERATE MONARCH

After Abdullah was assassinated, his son Talal reigned briefly. When it became obvious that the king's poor health would not allow him to rule effectively, Talal abdicated in favor of his son, Hussein. Still a teenager, Hussein would soon demonstrate maturity and wisdom beyond his years. From the outset he was a moderate monarch.

KING HUSSEIN

In historic time Jordan was an adolescent country, and now it was to be ruled by an adolescent monarch. The eighteen-year-old Prince Hussein was crowned king of the Hashemite Kingdom of Jordan on May 2, 1953. Pessimists predicted that the teenage king would soon be toppled or that he would become the puppet of some stronger power. Instead, he proved to be stubborn and perceptive enough to pursue paths of moderation. This sense of balance enabled him to survive in the volatile Middle East for nearly five decades.

He would achieve such longevity as a leader in part through reliance on a good Middle Eastern and European education, and in part by observing his grandfather Abdullah. Abdullah had favored Hussein and encouraged him to watch and learn from the king's interactions with his subjects.

As monarch, Abdullah, with the young Hussein seated nearby, received Jordanians of varied backgrounds and occupations: farmers of the Jordan River Valley, nomadic Bedouin, and Palestinians from the West Bank. Hussein grew to appreciate and understand Jordan's mix of cultures. His knowledge of the country and its people created an insightful and confident leader.

Hussein was to need this confidence to deal with his diverse subjects. According to author Helen Chapin Metz:

At its creation, Jordan was an artificial entity because inhabitants of northern Jordan have traditionally associated with Syria, those of southern Jordan have associated with the Arabian Peninsula, and those of western Jordan have identified with Palestinians in the West Bank.[10]

COPING WITH UNREST

In the early years of Hussein's reign over this diverse mix of people, peace proved elusive. Stateless Palestinian refugees who had fled to Jordan after the 1948–1949 fighting used the country as a base for guerrilla attacks on Israel. Israeli forces in turn raided Jordanian border towns to the extent that Hussein threatened to reconsider the truce established with Israel by his grandfather in 1949.

Internal stability proved as hard to achieve as peace with Israel. The displaced Palestinians, many in tent camps, accused Hussein of not doing enough for them, and elements in his government criticized his moderate position toward Israel, alleging that he did not care enough about the Palestinian cause. Resentful of the West's support of Israel, both groups charged Hussein with being a tool of Western nations, specifically Great Britain and America. In fact, Hussein still consulted with the British and received British subsidies to sustain his military.

Accusations that Hussein was a puppet of the West were fueled by Egyptian leader Gamal Abdel Nasser, a champion of Arab nationalism, an enemy of the West, and a friend to the communist Soviet Union, which supplied him with arms. One of several Arab leaders vying for dominance in the Arab world, Nasser had seized control of Egypt in a military coup in 1952. His rival for Arab leadership was Faisal of Iraq, Hussein's cousin. Hussein and Faisal had formed a pact

Eighteen-year-old Hussein assumed the throne upon his father's abdication.

Cousins King Faisal of Iraq (left) and King Hussein review Arab Legion troops in Amman, Jordan.

called the Arab Federation. However, in a plot believed to have been hatched by Nasser, Faisal would be murdered by officers in his own military in 1958. A similar coup against Hussein failed. Nasser continued to seek ways to undermine the moderate Jordanian monarch in the Arab world, where anti-Western feelings ran high. Insults against Hussein were broadcast daily from Cairo.

Before his death Faisal had agreed to the Baghdad Pact. Intended to contain the spread of communism in the region, this proposal by Western powers called for a Middle East defense system coordinated by Britain. Besides Iraq, the countries of Turkey, Iran, and Pakistan signed on. However, a furious Nasser denounced the pact, which he believed smacked of Western colonialism, and formed a competing rival for Arab leadership, the United Arab Republic, an alliance of Egypt, Syria, and Saudi Arabia.

Pondering his own move, Hussein appointed a prime minister who supported Jordan's signing the Baghdad Pact.

This led to riots in both the East and West Bank by Palestinians who hated the West for its support of Israel. Hussein used diplomacy to quickly strike a deal with Nasser in which Nasser agreed to stop the radio attacks on Hussein, and Hussein agreed not to join the Baghdad Pact.

Hussein then promptly called for British help in quelling the riots against him, which had reached the stage of a serious revolt. Britain sent military support in the form of paratroops and Vampire jet fighters from nearby Cyprus, while Hussein's own army used tear gas and guns to clear the streets.

DISTANCING FROM BRITAIN

In the end, to keep peace and to strengthen his bonds with other Arab leaders, Hussein put an end to British involvement in Jordan's affairs. He dismissed his old friend John Glubb, the British officer who still served as commander of the Jordanian army. With this act, Hussein forfeited British monetary aid, which at that time made up about half of Jordan's budget. But, as Hussein had hoped, approving Arab nations promised Jordan some financial aid.

Arab leaders (seated left to right) King Hussein, King Saud of Saudi Arabia, Egyptian president Gamal Nasser, and Syrian Premier Sabri Assali sign the Jordan Aid Agreement providing financial aid to Jordan.

Still, Hussein did not give up Western aid entirely. Despite not signing the Baghdad Pact, Hussein continued to take an anticommunist stance. His rejection of communism was routed in his strong Islamic faith, which states that all obedience is owed to God, or Allah. By contrast, in atheist communism, all obedience is due the state. Hussein's position brought aid from the United States, which saw Jordan as an ally in its fight to contain the spread of communism.

PROGRESS FOR JORDAN

With the crisis of revolt averted, Jordan could take advantage of its admission to the United Nations in 1955. Hussein could now receive UN aid and join in trade agreements favorable to Jordan. With aid from America and his Arab neighbors, and with revenue from an income tax he enacted, Hussein started government-sponsored construction projects, highways, airlines, and communication systems. He improved the port of Aqaba to make it more accessible to foreign commerce. Work began on the Ibn Hasna Dam, which was to store irrigation water and provide a wide area of the country with electricity generated by a hydroelectric plant.

But, in spite of Jordan's progress in improving the lives of its citizens, the Palestinians living there still wanted their own country, with its own government, established in their lost lands west of the Jordan River. Hussein had granted them citizenship, the right to hold land, and mid- and lower-level government positions, but that was not enough. Egypt was still advocating the total elimination of Israel as the only way that peace could be achieved in the Middle East.

Hussein rejected that concept, and his views remained moderate: The Middle East had seen Jews and Arabs live in peace before and could do so again. He did not believe the Palestinians could regain their homeland by fighting, and argued that negotiation and compromise were their only viable option.

MEETING DANGER WITH COURAGE

Hussein's moderation made him many enemies. In the late 1950s Hussein had to contend with uprisings among his subjects and attempts on his life, some thought to be at Nasser's instigation. During his reign, Hussein would survive eleven assassination attempts.

In the 1960s, Hussein showed he had a true capacity to forgive those who disliked him. He put his efforts into forg-

ASSASSINATION ATTEMPTS

King Hussein reigned in a volatile environment. His rule spanned five Arab-Israeli wars, Jordan's civil war with Palestinian guerrillas, and repeated assassination attempts, eleven of which are documented. Historians attribute at least some of the assassination conspiracies to Egyptian president Nasser and his sympathizers.

The first threat to the king's life was in 1957. Plotters incited a rebellion at an army base at Az Zarqa, expecting the king to be shot when he arrived to restore order. Trusting the loyalty of his Bedouin officers, Hussein stood up in his car and dared any disloyal officer to shoot him. None did.

Subsequent attempts took many forms. On November 10, 1958, Syrian MiG-17s tried to force Hussein, piloting his Dove aircraft, to land in Damascus. He turned the controls over to his copilot, who outraced the pursuers to reach Jordan and safety.

A few years later, Hussein's cook was discovered experimenting on palace cats with doses of poison; fifteen of the animals died. Hussein's housekeeper, pouring the contents of a bottle of the king's nose drops into another container, noticed spilled drops were corroding the sink. Someone had laced them with acid. Hussein's decision to make an unscheduled visit to a new site at the University of Amman caused him to miss a bomb explosion in his prime minister's office that killed eleven people.

After a period of relative calm, the civil war brought more assassination attempts. On July 9, 1970, Hussein, accompanied by a motorcade of six armed Land Rovers, drove toward Amman from his summer villa. The group rounded a curve into an ambush of Palestinian commandos firing Russian 50mm machine guns at the king. He fired back from his car window, then opened the door and escaped by rolling into a ditch.

Later one of Hussein's drivers was exposed as a Palestinian commando. A second cook, arrested in possession of a hand grenade, also tried to poison the king.

ing a more united Arab front within the Arab world and within his own country. He made progress: More Palestinians were moving out of the refugee camps, finding work and living normal lives in city suburbs. It seemed, according to journalist Sandra Mackey, "that Hussein, given enough time, might turn Palestinians into loyal Jordanians."[11]

However, a new problem was about to burden Hussein. Nasser and the Arab League had organized the Palestine Liberation Organization (PLO). This coordinating council of various organizations of Palestinian refugees was committed to using force to destroy Israel and return Palestine to the Palestinians. But because the Palestinian National Charter of 1964 forbade the PLO from causing internal trouble in any Arab country, Hussein allowed it to headquarter in Jordan.

Trouble developed there almost at once. The PLO moved freely among refugee camps, taxing the inhabitants, training soldiers, and distributing guns. Worse, the PLO formed the radical Al-Fatah, a guerrilla organization, and launched secret strikes against Israel from Jordan.

Fearful of Israeli reprisals, Hussein ordered his army to the border to intercept PLO guerrillas. Although the action was largely effective, an angry Israel sent forces to destroy the West Bank village of Samu on November 13, 1966. Eighteen of its Palestinian residents, subjects of King Hussein, were killed.

Many of Jordan's Palestinian citizens took to the streets, outraged when Hussein refused to retaliate against Israel. Hussein feared full-scale civil war as much as war with Israel. To make

Members of the PLO guerrilla organization, Al-Fatah, march during military training.

matters more difficult for the king, Nasser was pushing for a war against Israel. Hussein's subjects, especially those on the West Bank, wanted Hussein to back Nasser in the event of war. If Nasser did go to war against the Israelis and Hussein did not support Nasser, civil war in Jordan would surely come.

To avoid it, on May 30, 1967, Hussein flew to Egypt and signed a defense pact with his old opponent Nasser. Under their five-year agreement, Hussein placed his military forces under Egyptian command in the event of war. Hussein received a hero's welcome from his delighted Palestinian subjects when he returned to Jordan.

WAR WITH ISRAEL

The Arabs and Israelis would not wait long for open conflict. Believing that Arabs were planning to attack Israel, Israeli forces launched a preemptive attack on Egypt, Syria, and Jordan on June 5, 1967. Contradictory orders from the pessimistic Egyptian commander and a more aggressive Hussein led to confusion among their forces as to when to fight and when to retreat. After only three days of fighting, Hussein lost both Jerusalem and the West Bank.

Israel had tried to get a message to Hussein to prevent his involvement in the war, but it had failed to reach him in time. In any event he had already made his costly agreement with Nasser. Author Sandra Mackey writes of the catastrophic outcome for Hussein: "His need to evince loyalty to the Arab cause had cost him the legacy of Abdullah. Populous Arab towns like Bethlehem, Hebron, Ramallah, and Nablus passed from Jordan to Israel. And Jerusalem, including the sacred Dome of the Rock, slid from the grasp of the Hashemites."[12]

The war and subsequent loss of the West Bank devastated Jordan. Hussein had lost the fertile croplands of the West Bank while gaining some two hundred thousand more refugees.

TROUBLE WITH THE PLO

Another effect of the 1967 Arab war with Israel, dubbed the Six-Day War, was that it gained world recognition and new

King Hussein signed a defense pact with President Gamal Nasser (pictured) placing Jordan military forces under Egyptian command in the event of war with Israel.

members for the PLO. The PLO ignored UN cease-fire orders and ordered its guerrilla recruits to launch attacks against Israel from Jordan. PLO chairman Yasir Arafat's fully armed troops openly strode through Amman, going into homes and hotels to collect money for PLO activities.

The Palestinian commando movement included several factions, some beyond even Arafat's control. The leftist Popular Front for the Liberation of Palestine (PFLP) hated Hussein for his moderate attitude toward Israel and the West. PFLP commandos hijacked international airline flights, forcing pilots to land in Jordan. Such acts of terrorism demonstrated these groups' hostility toward anything Western or pro-Western, and their contempt for Jordan's government.

Hussein's proud, largely Bedouin army was clearly frustrated by his refusal to order his troops to move against the PLO. He knew mutiny might occur and he would lose the loyalty of his army if he did not challenge the PLO soon.

Finally, on September 16, 1970, in the month known afterward as Black September, Hussein declared a state of martial law. He ordered his army to move against the PLO guerrillas, and by July 1971 the PLO had been driven out of Jordan.

Hussein assured those Palestinians who had not fought against him that normal life could resume. He continued to lobby in international forums for the establishment of a Palestinian homeland. He also continued to insist that that goal could not be obtained by war, only by negotiation.

ATTEMPTS TO RECLAIM THE WEST BANK

Hussein would try to get back the West Bank and Jerusalem by negotiation and political maneuvers as well. He entered into discussions that led to UN Resolution 242 calling for Israel to return occupied lands it gained in 1967 for recognition of its right to remain within secure borders. In 1972 Hussein proposed the formation of the United Arab Kingdom. This federation would be a combination of the East and West Banks as autonomous provinces with separate councils, under the jurisdiction of the Hashemite kingdom with a federal capital in Amman. The Arab world resented his proposal, seeing it as an attempt by Hussein to rule over lands that should be controlled by independent Palestinians.

This resentment led to a resolution proposed at the 1974 Arab Summit Conference in Rabat, Morocco, naming the PLO official representative for any future Palestinian territories. A humiliated and disappointed Hussein agreed to the resolution. Journalist Sandra Mackey quotes Hussein's statement of his commitment to Arab unity: "There is an Arab verse which says . . . Where my tribe goes, I go. . . . As part of the Arab nation, ever seeking its unity, I go with the general consensus . . . regardless of any previous feelings."[13] By agreeing, however reluctantly, to the PLO's representing Palestinians, he again improved his strained relations with other Arab leaders. They believed he had relinquished any official claim to the West Bank.

But, in truth, Hussein simply could not accept the loss of the West Bank. In the years following the Rabat Conference, he reorganized Jordan's political institutions in a way that left

ROYAL MARRIAGES

King Hussein's domestic life at times proved as stormy as his public one. His first marriage, in 1955, was to his cousin Princess Dina. They divorced after two years and two children. In 1961 he married Antoinette Gardiner, the daughter of a Jordanian-based British general. Their marriage brought two sons and twin daughters. Hussein divorced Gardiner in 1972 and married Alia Toukan, the daughter of a West Bank family. They had a daughter in 1974 and a son in 1975. Hussein grieved deeply following her 1977 death in a helicopter crash.

Hussein's final marriage in 1978 was to a woman fifteen years his junior. Lisa Halaby, mature beyond her years, was the daughter of an American

businessman of Arab descent. When they married, Hussein renamed her Noor al Hussein, the Light of Hussein. Queen Noor bore him four children. She reared their children as well as the young children of Queen Alia. She was devoted to the king and their marriage ended only with his death in 1999.

Queen Noor and King Hussein on their wedding day.

open the possibility of reuniting the West Bank with Jordan. For example, he amended the constitution, giving himself power to suspend elections for the House of Representatives because such elections would have taken place on the East Bank alone, thus signifying the final separation of the West Bank from Jordan. While he favored establishment of a Palestinian homeland, he hoped to see a Palestinian homeland whose people would ultimately vote for some kind of joint government with Jordan.

In the 1970s Hussein focused on restoration of the West Bank to Jordan, peace in the Middle East, and rebuilding those parts of Jordan that had been devastated by the Six-Day War. His economy improved as financial aid from Kuwait, Saudi Arabia, and the United States reduced debts resulting from war and the subsequent waves of refugees. Jordan and Israel also worked out a policy that allowed many Palestinians to return to the West Bank.

REJECTING THE CAMP DAVID ACCORDS

In 1979 Jordan's improved relationships with both Egypt and the United States became strained when Hussein refused to join in a peace settlement between Egypt and Israel, brokered by the United States, called the Camp David Accords. Hussein, who had not been invited to the negotiations, felt the agreement was far too vague about the future of the West Bank. According to journalist Milton Viorst, "To the Palestinians, Camp David was a devils' bargain by which Israel restored Sinai to Egypt in return for legitimation of its own rule on the West Bank and in Gaza."[14] Hussein's rejection of the Camp David Accords brought him solidly back into the Arab fold; all Arab leaders outside Egypt rejected the Camp David Accords along with Hussein.

As a result, he received significant aid from his oil-rich neighbors and many Jordanians and Jordanian Palestinians found work in the Saudi Arabian oil fields. These expatriate workers sent money to their families at home, who improved the local economy through spending. The workers' pay, subject to Jordanian taxation, was a direct boon to the Jordanian treasury; the petro-boom of the 1970s, when oil prices soared, seemed a promising time.

When war broke out between Iraq and Iran in 1980, Jordan's movement toward prosperity was unaffected. Hussein

supported Iraq and made economic gains for Jordan by
opening Aqaba to replace besieged Iraqi ports.

SEEKING INTERNATIONAL AID

Other sources of unrest continued to plague the Middle East
in the 1980s. Israel invaded Lebanon in 1982 and appeared to
be taking a more aggressive stance everywhere in the region.
Seeking a diplomatic solution, American president Ronald
Reagan pushed a proposal that Jordan assume control of the
West Bank in return for Arab recognition of Israel. Hussein
jumped to its support, but the PLO would not agree.

With the failure of the Reagan plan, the United States became less willing to provide financial help to Jordan. So, although not procommunist, the flexible Hussein turned not
only to the West, particularly France, but also to the Soviet
Union for military supplies as well as for help with Palestinian issues.

*Israel's invasion of
Lebanon in 1982 added
to the unrest in the
Middle East.*

RELINQUISHING CLAIMS TO THE WEST BANK

Throughout everything, Hussein kept alive his dream of regaining the West Bank. In 1984 he reconvened the Jordanian Parliament, half of whose members were Palestinian. Thus, Hussein maintained a relationship with both Palestinian and Jordanian Arabs. In March 1986, the Jordanian legislature increased membership in its House of Representatives from 60 to 142, with 71 seats to Palestinians. After negotiations with Israel, Hussein entered into a $1.3 billion investment plan to help reconstruct the West Bank.

In 1985, Hussein attempted to establish a pact with Arafat that would allow them to jointly pursue a peace initiative in which Israel might trade land for peace. However, Hussein's attempts to negotiate with Israel failed because factions in the PLO would not endorse any agreement between the Jordanian monarch and Israel. As he had from the beginning, Arafat continued to refuse to recognize Israel as called for in UN Resolution 242.

Then in 1987, extremists foiled hopes for Jordanian leadership of the West Bank. Palestinians in the West Bank began the intifada, an uprising that commenced on December 9, 1987. There, stone-throwing Palestinians fought against armed Israeli soldiers. Sporadic clashes continued for months with no sign of settlement. Soon, sympathetic Palestinians on the East Bank began to riot as well. Hussein now found even his East Bank kingdom in jeopardy.

On July 31, 1988, Hussein officially renounced any Jordanian claim to the West Bank. In doing so, he shifted all responsibility for its future return to the Palestinians to the PLO. Jordan also stopped providing the West Bank with development funds.

But relinquishing hopes for the West Bank did not mean Hussein's monarchy was less vulnerable to criticism. His loyal Jordanian constituency was now shrinking. Both Jordanians and Palestinians, including members of the usually loyal army, were unhappy with declining living standards brought about by economic recession in the late 1980s. Elections in 1989 showed the growing strength of Islamic fundamentalists, not great supporters of Hussein.

THE GULF WAR

Worse was to come. The 1990 Iraqi invasion of pro-Western Kuwait, which led to the Persian Gulf War, placed Jordan in a political nightmare. Most Arab countries opposed Iraq's act of aggression. Saudi Arabia, where the Kuwaiti royal family had fled for sanctuary, invited the United States to assist in protecting Saudi territory from the threat of further Iraqi aggression. Hussein sided with Iraq, as he had done during Iraq's war with Iran. The neighboring countries' history included financial support from Iraq to Jordan.

Therefore, Hussein allowed Iraq to use Aqaba and Jordanian trucks to carry supplies to its war front. This decision was popular with his subjects, but drew criticism from the international community.

QUEEN NOOR

Her Majesty Queen Noor, of Arab-American descent, was born Lisa Najeeb Halaby on August 23, 1951. Her father served as head of the Federal Aviation Administration under President John F. Kennedy. She graduated from Princeton University in 1974 with a degree in architecture and urban planning. She then worked for Royal Jordanian Airline as director of planning and design projects until her marriage to King Hussein on June 15, 1978.

From the start of her reign she actively worked to nurture Arab-Western friendships and the well-being of Jordanian citizens. Her efforts have included promoting the health and education of children by the establishment of immunization campaigns, a children's hospital, and scholarships for promising children from poor, remote areas of Jordan. The queen also worked to improve the status of Jordanian women.

Attuned to the need for unity among nations of the Arab world, she convened the first Arab Children's Congress to promote understanding of shared culture and history. Along with others she founded the Jerash Festival for Culture and Art and Jordan's National Music Conservatory, both of which showcase international talent. She received the UN Environment Program Global 500 Award for her activism in international conservation organizations.

Queen Noor is a devout Muslim convert and is fluent in Arabic, English, and French. Although no longer reigning queen, she remains active in humanitarian causes.

Queen Noor visits with Jordanian citizens.

After ruling for forty-six years, King Hussein succumbed to cancer in 1999.

When Hussein did agree to observe the UN embargo against Iraq, it cost him hundreds of millions of dollars in lost income from trade. That, combined with the wartime collapse of tourism, loss of economic aid from the furious Saudi Arabia, Kuwait, and the United States, and loss of Jordanian jobs in the Saudi oil fields cost Jordan about $2 billion.

After the war's end, Hussein started the hard work of rebuilding relationships with disaffected Arab neighbors. Once again, Hussein was successful in establishing ties with other Arab countries, and financial assistance from those countries came into Jordan.

In 1991, Hussein played a role in Middle East peace talks. After all, both his enemies and friends respected him as a longtime player on the Middle Eastern stage, and his country's location continued to be central to the region's politics. But the leader who could survive political attacks and assassination attempts could not go on forever. After a hard-fought battle with cancer, King Hussein died in 1999.

Hussein had proven himself a stubborn, smart, and courageous leader. His subjects and people throughout the Middle East respected him even when they did not agree with him. A statesman who typified the ideal of honor, King Hussein clearly proved the wisdom of being a moderate monarch.

Daily Life

Jordan is a modern nation whose people's daily lives remain influenced by traditional Arab Muslim ways. Sixty percent of Jordan's citizens are Palestinian Arabs who were, or are descended from, inhabitants of the Middle East region called Palestine that was under British control from 1922 until 1948. Most of Jordan's Palestinian Arabs arrived as refugees fleeing the West Bank during and after the Arab-Israeli wars of 1948 and 1967. The Palestinians tend to be educated, sophisticated people. Many gravitated as soon as they could from refugee camps to urban centers like Jordan's capital, Amman. By the late 1980s they made up 60 to 80 percent of Amman's population and most of the city's entrepreneurs.

The rest of the population is mostly native Arab, divided between the Bedouin, nomadic people of the desert, and the fellahin, settled villager-farmers. There is a small (about 2 percent) minority of Circassians and Chechens from the Caucasus of Russia and immigrant Armenians.

Seventy percent of Jordan's population live in urban centers like Amman, the capital of Jordan (pictured).

53

About 96 percent of Jordan's population is Sunni Muslim and the remaining 4 percent is Christian. Most of the Christian population is Greek Orthodox, or Greek Catholic; the remainder are members of Roman Catholic and various Protestant denominations. The majority of the Christian population is urban.

The influx of Palestinian refugees coincided with the movement of rural Arabs to the city seeking advantages such as better education for their children and better jobs in service industries or in the government civil service. These developments, combined with a high birth rate, caused explosive growth in the population of Amman, from thirty thousand in 1943 to 1.7 million by the year 2000. Such migration to urban centers has created significant social change.

URBAN LIFE

According to Middle East scholar Helen Chapin Metz, writing of Amman in the 1970s, "New urban areas, dotted with lavish stone villas and supermarkets and boutiques supplied with expensive imported items, coexisted with overcrowded areas where a jumble of buildings housed the multitudes of the lower-middle class and the poor."[15]

City life, more modernized than village or nomadic life, nonetheless retains a distinct Arab/Islamic flavor. Urban Jordanians, nearly 70 percent of the population, enjoy theater, concerts, opera, ballet, and cinema. Internet cafes in Amman serve espresso to patrons using computer terminals. However, American professor Michael Beard, who taught literature at the University of Amman in 1997, describes the city's appearance as austere because the buildings are constructed almost uniformly of granitelike stone traditionally used in the Middle East. Beard also notes the mixture of Western and traditional styles of dress: "Women will often wear western dress, but usually with head-scarves."[16]

Journalist Milton Viorst writes of modern Amman:

It is a city of open spaces and well-washed streets, of soaring high-rises and superhighways that leap across ravines, of nightclubs and flower gardens and neon signs. Occasionally a hooded woman glides by, the hem

Two women in traditional dress traverse Amman's busy sidewalks with a small child.

of her robe brushing the sidewalk. Now and then the perfume of Oriental spices enriches a breeze. But a more common sight is a teenager in blue jeans on a motorbike, and exhaust fumes are a more pervasive odor.[17]

Amman's population rises early, usually before dawn, for prayer. By 7:00 A.M. the streets are filled with vehicles, many privately owned, many part of a public transportation system in which taxis are plentiful and inexpensive, as are buses and smaller shuttle-style vans. In the outer parts of this sprawling city, shepherds driving herds of cows or sheep are a common sight.

Lunch breaks are long, at least two hours. Businesses often shut their doors at midday, then reopen in the afternoon until late evening. City dwellers congregate in shops to socialize as well as to buy goods.

When they are not at work, urban Jordanians enjoy playing and watching soccer and basketball, and horse and camel racing are popular spectator sports. At home, watching television is a relaxing pastime; Jordanians may be as knowledgeable as their American counterparts about popular Western programs. Families frequently enjoy picnics on outings in the many local parks sprinkled throughout urban centers.

VILLAGE LIFE

Only about 5 or 6 percent of Jordan's population is truly nomadic, so the remaining 25 percent of the population outside cities are villagers, known as fellahin. Their lives largely depend on agriculture, and revolve around long-held traditions of community and family.

While the tradition of extended family living under one roof is becoming less common in Jordan's cities, it is still the norm in the less prosperous villages. In rural Jordan, numerous relatives live in modest houses of just one or two rooms. Fellahin homes are generally made of stone, cinderblock, or whitewashed mud brick. Usually, only one member of a family owns a car, which is readily shared with any relative in need of transportation. Fortunately, most places in a typical village can be reached on foot.

In the Islamic countryside, as in urban centers, villagers rise early for prayer. Their midday break is a long one. They return to work until evening, when many head home to watch television or visit friends.

 JIHAD: CODE OF ETHICS

To Muslims, jihad refers to the perpetual struggle for the triumph of the word of God on earth. Many Westerners associate the term only with the violent holy wars conducted by the Muslim state against nonbelievers. That state is not a geographic entity, but the community of Islam, to which Muslims everywhere belong. Each member of that community is equally bound by a binding code of conduct found in the Koran, the sacred text of Islam.

To most Muslims, jihad sets forth a general duty, and regulates how one human being relates to another. Through jihad, Islam encourages generosity, fairness, honesty, respect, and prescribed behavior within the family. It also forbids adultery, gambling, usury (charging interest for loans), and the consumption of certain foods as well as alcohol.

Larger villages tend to be concentrated in the northwest corner of Jordan and in the Jordan River Valley. The more fertile and well irrigated the land, the greater the village size. Family members go from the village to work in their fields. There they grow vegetables, fruits, grains, and some tobacco. Farming methods are modern, with tractors, combines, and sophisticated irrigation systems a common sight. At festivals celebrating the harvest since ancient times, however, families join in singing traditional songs, dancing, and feasting.

In villages in less fertile areas, agriculture has declined as a way of life and with it, the older generation's traditional control of family finances. Younger men gain financial independence through other forms of labor, such as mining or work in factories. They may also migrate to other countries. Nevertheless, as Jordanian men, they usually remain deeply respectful of and involved in the welfare and lives of their families.

THE BEDOUIN

The nomadic Bedouin exist in all desert areas of Jordan as they do throughout the deserts of the Middle East. A proud people, they adhere to tradition more strongly than other groups in the Jordanian population.

Though the word *Bedu* literally means "nomad," not all Bedouin are completely nomadic. Truly nomadic Bedouin tribes have specific winter and summer camping areas, where they graze their herds of goats, sheep, or camels. When fodder runs out, the tribe moves on. Many nomads are found in the Bawaadi, the desert region east of a line from Al Maqaafa to Ma'an.

Seminomadic groups raise sheep and goats, but engage in agriculture as well as herding. They move only short distances within a given area. For example, many Bedouin farm in the Jordan River Valley but move their herds into the hills in summer to avoid the intense heat of the lower settlements.

Groups labeled semisedentary are even more rooted in agriculture. Parts of a semisedentary group move with the sheep and goats in search of new fodder. The rest of the group stay in permanent housing and cultivate the fields.

Many Bedouin prefer the old ways and continue to live a nomadic life despite the declining resources available in the desert.

Many Bedouin are now sedentary. The government encourages them to forgo both the freedoms and the hardships of the desert dweller's lifestyle. Disciplined and accustomed to codes of authority, many excel as officers in the military. The Jordanian government, aware that the resources of the desert have become depleted due to overgrazing, offers to provide education for children and housing for the approximately forty thousand Bedouin who remain nomadic. However, despite the difficulties and dangers of the harsh desert, many Bedouin simply prefer the old ways.

Author Milton Viorst provides a glimpse of those who did give up nomadic wandering as he describes a visit to the Bani Hamida tribe, some thirty-five hundred strong, who now live in a series of villages near Ma'an in sight of the Dead Sea:

> Though their cement block houses had electricity and water, many said they preferred sleeping bedouin-style, in tents which they pitched in adjacent fields. Most of

the men held menial jobs in nearby towns. About half of the women wove traditional rugs as part of a self-help project sponsored by Save the Children, an American development agency. A few families had planted olive trees, and some tended sheep and goats, but the dry, rocky soil yielded very little for the handful that farmed. None of the Bani Hamida, not even the children, wore Western clothes . . . but neither were the women veiled. The children all attended school . . . and many went on to the university. The older inhabitants readily shared memories with me of life on the move with camels, but acknowledged that their current life, with radios and clinics and cars, was far less onerous.[18]

Though the Bedouin have largely adopted a more settled lifestyle, their timeless tradition of prizing the family and its honor are reflected in all levels of Jordanian culture.

BEDOUIN INFLUENCE ON CHARACTER AND FAMILY
In significant ways the roles and values of both men and women in Jordan have their origins in the ancient nomadic peoples of the desert. The Bedouin have played a large part in shaping the character and family-based culture of Jordanians, derived from the Bedouin tribal system and its values. Although tribes also have existed in Jordanian villages, the tribal system remains strongest among the Bedouin.

Bedouin families, usually claiming a common ancestor, group together to form a clan. They select a leader, or sheik. Clans may join other clans to form tribes, headed by selected individuals in a pyramid of power. Confederations of tribes form alliances that endure, sometimes for generations, sometimes for shorter periods for specific purposes.

Tribal affiliations have had influences on Jordanian political elections conducted since Jordan's adoption of its 1952 constitution. The men and women of a particular tribe have followed their sheiks' endorsement of certain politicians and vote accordingly. With the migration of many Bedouin to the cities, sheiks' power over voters is lessening, although their influence may still be significant, depending on the tribe.

Bedouins have traditionally placed great emphasis on honor (*ird*). A slight or injury to one tribal member was considered an injury to all. And all had to answer for the behavior of each single member. According to Middle East expert

HONOR CRIMES

Traditionally, the male members of a Jordanian family have a duty to defend its honor. This obligation has contributed to a situation in Jordan that many would like to change: tolerance of honor crimes. In a particular instance that has drawn attention in modern times, if a woman disgraces her family by sexual misconduct, a male relative, often her brother, can act to restore the family honor by killing her.

Article 340 of Jordan's penal code exempts from punishment men who kill female relatives found or even suspected to have committed adultery. It also provides for the imposition of light sentences on those who kill unmarried female relatives who have sexual relations. About 25 percent—twenty by actual count—of all murders that take place in Jordan each year are honor crimes.

The government has twice submitted a draft law to repeal Article 340, but the lower house of parliament has voted against it. Deputies in parliament charged that the government was submitting to Western attempts to influence Jordanian society.

The issue will not go away, however. Senior members of the royal family, including Prince Ghazi, the king's cousin, have spoken against Article 340. In February 2000, King Abdullah's brother, Prince Ali, led a march of some three thousand Jordanians to parliament to demand that its members revoke Article 340.

Helen Chapin Metz, "Honor inhered in the family or tribe and in the individual as the representative of the family or tribe. Slights were to be erased by appropriate revenge or through mediation to reach reconciliation based on adequate recompense."[19]

The concept of honor infuses other aspects of life. According to journalist Sandra Mackey:

Even the Arabs' famous hospitality is an exercise in honor. . . . In the wasteland of the desert, a man pursuing a straying camel could easily become separated from the protective circle of his kin and tribe. . . . Under the tribes' commonly accepted rules of hospitality, a wanderer coming upon a camp entered as an honored guest. The rule applied to everyone, including the son of a hated enemy or the target of bitter revenge. But mere protection was not enough. Generosity in food was also demanded. Poverty, even at its meanest, did not excuse a man from fulfilling the sublime duty of hospitality—to shelter and feed a guest for three days.[20]

THE ALL-IMPORTANT FAMILY

To city dweller and rural villager alike, family and family honor are traditionally all-important. Middle East expert Sandra Mackey writes of family, "It is life itself. For it is from the family that an Arab draws his identity and his security."[21]

Kinship in Jordan is determined patrilinially, that is, by the male line. Children belong to their father's family rather than their mother's.

Jordanians rely on family members for financial support, employment leads, social introductions (including introductions to potential spouses), mediation or protection in conflicts, child care, domestic help, social identity, and emotional nurturing. In return, the individual owes his or her family loyalty and reciprocal support.

An Arab woman's traditional role has been to bear and raise children.

Although movement into urban centers has resulted in more families living in nuclear households, homes filled with extended family are still the norm in Jordan. An extended family will include at least three generations: grandparents, parents, and children. Unmarried sisters, in-laws, or other relatives may live in the home as well.

FAMILY ROLES

The household roles of men, women, and children are set in tradition and religious tenets. According to Islam, women should be subservient to their husbands. Therefore, the father wields considerable authority. Except when they had to work to help support the family, women's historic role has been to manage the household and bear and rear children. Especially in urban centers, men customarily provide sole support for the family. All men have more personal freedom than women, but younger men defer to such male elders as grandfathers, fathers, or uncles. However, decisions about important matters such as education, marriage, and employment are subject to family discussions.

In a household with several married women, older women have considerable control over younger wives. This has led some young wives to prefer life in households consisting only of themselves, their husbands, and their children. However, in these circumstances, they may find themselves subject to more direct control by their husbands and without female relatives' help in managing the home.

Older women also rule over the household's children and adolescents. Children receive much loving attention from affectionate family adults. They are indulged while toddlers, but by age four or five are expected to start assuming some chores. Spanking and severe scolding is not considered inconsistent with the deep love bestowed on them by the family.

The elderly in Jordan are entitled to pension payments that make the aged somewhat less dependent on their children, but the cost of living and traditional practices still mean that generations often live together.

 ## RELIGIOUS COURTS

The religion of Islam does not separate church and state, and makes no distinction between religious and secular law. Muslims believe that Allah revealed the rules of proper behavior to Muhammad and followers of Islam must submit to those holy injunctions.

The Jordanian justice system has incorporated religious courts, granting them specific jurisdiction over personal issues and disputes in religious communities. For example, the religious courts settle disputes concerning marriage, divorce, alimony, child custody, guardianship, and inheritance, as well as community endowments.

There are two types of religious courts. Muslim courts are called sharia. One judge, a qadi, presides over each sharia and applies Islamic law as the basis for his decisions. A second category of religious court handles cases within Jordan's minority Christian community. Three judges, usually ordained religious leaders, preside over each Christian court. Their judgments are rendered on the basis of canon law, applying Greek Orthodox, Melchite, Roman Catholic, and Anglican interpretations.

To perpetuate the vitally important family, everyone is expected to marry. The right marital age for girls, until recently the midteens, has risen to the early twenties. Men tend to marry at twenty-six or twenty-eight. Grown children live at home until they marry, or in the case of sons, even afterward. While living at home, children are expected to obey their parents.

WOMEN'S LIVES

Although traditional influences remain strong, life for Jordanian women is changing with the nation's modernization and exposure to Western influences. In fundamentalist, traditional Muslim households women are confined to the home and wear the chador, a combination veil/scarf that covers the head and most of the face, as well as long, loose-fitting garments that reveal nothing of the female figure.

These women have enrolled in trade school and are learning how to make picture frames.

In the last four decades, however, many Jordanian women have been more active outside the home and have increasingly sought greater freedom and equality, including the choice of Western-style clothing. Education has played the greatest role in this transformation. In the 1980s girls' enrollment in Jordanian schools equaled that of boys. Educated females have since tended to put off marriage in favor of a career for a few years after graduation.

Today, couples tend to choose each other romantically, seeking spouses with shared education and social status, instead of entering into traditional family-arranged marriages. However, every Jordanian woman still lives under the Islamic decree that she must marry her father's brother's son unless the young man releases her from that obligation.

Islamic law affects married life in other ways. For example, though a man may have four wives at one time, a woman may have only one husband. The process of divorce is easy for men, who only have to repeat "I divorce thee" three times to the woman. Women have to prove serious and specific cause before authorities grant them a divorce.

In practice, only wealthy men can afford multiple wives. Likewise, men do not choose divorce hastily, as they may have to forfeit their wife's dowry or pay a high separation settlement. However, as other men succeed in well-paying careers, some do take up and dispose of wives at will, leaving some women destitute and deprived of their children.

Still, the number of women working outside the home continues to increase and women have risen to cabinet-level positions. The royal family does not favor fundamentalism in religion and so encourages women in the workforce. The least societal resistance is accorded to women in accepted female employment roles such as teaching, nursing, and secretarial work. Such conformity to traditional roles applies to women serving in the armed forces; most serve in secretarial, administrative, communications, or medical capacities.

Perhaps one reason that Jordanian women have progressed, aside from King Hussein's encouraging approach, has been the tendency, especially during the oil boom of the 1970s and early 80s, of men to go abroad to work. Sometimes wife and children would see their husband and father only once or twice a year. While many women waited for their husbands to return to make major decisions, they often lived alone with their children, making many independent decisions on a daily basis.

FAMILY HOMES

Among Bedouin as well as other family groups, housing varies according to a family's level of prosperity. The very wealthy may live in elegant modern villas, often of stone, but most live in modest traditional houses.

The design of a traditional Muslim house involves rectangular dwelling units organized around an inner courtyard. The exterior is plain and windowless. Courtyard houses are frequently grouped into a walled complex shared by an extended family. Expansion occurs as the family grows. Once all the land is used, second and third stories are added to accommodate new family members. The open-air interior courtyard allows outdoor activity while offering privacy and protection from wind and sun. It also functions as a sink for cool air at night. This type of architecture, with its plain exterior and inner courtyard, expresses the Arab wish to exclude the outside world while protecting the family and its inner life inside.

An Arab man sits in front of his home, a typical cement-block house.

The less prosperous reside in small cement-block houses, consisting of perhaps only one room, or boxy housing of brick or wood. The small percentage of remaining nomadic Bedouin of the desert still dwell in woven goat hair tents.

Traditionally, both urban and rural homes of the well-to-do have separate men's and women's areas: the reception room, where men entertain male friends, and the women's section, or haram, where males (other than relatives or servants) are forbidden. Small houses lack space for segregation by gender; in the one- or two-room dwellings of poor rural areas, men and women socialize together in the house.

For all Jordanians, regardless of income level, modernization is a fact of life as people move in increasing numbers to

EDUCATION

Improving education has been a priority of the Jordanian government for many years. Education has brought about changes in lifestyles of women, aided in the shift to sedentary life for Bedouins, and helped curtail the 25 to 30 percent unemployment rate that forces many Jordanian husbands and fathers out of the country to find work.

Jordan's educational system has come a long way since the country's birth in 1921, when there were only twenty-five religious schools that provided a limited education. Today, the literacy rate has reached 86.6 percent. A gap between men and women exists, but is narrowing: 93.4 percent of males and 79.4 percent of females are literate. Similarly, the gap between urban and rural literacy rates has been closing. Rural areas, such as the Ma'an region, have traditionally lagged behind because the nomadic tribes did not make formal education a priority. Now, throughout the country, education is free and compulsory for elementary students.

In the 1970s and 1980s, the government recognized that Jordan's universities were turning out professionals and academics when what the country needed most was skilled technical labor. It addressed the problem by establishing community colleges. In these two-year schools, students can earn degrees in such fields as social services, education, computer science, communications, transportation, and paramedical technologies. Students can continue their studies at universities, well equipped to secure employment within the country. Thus, education is helping Jordanian families reach not only a more modern but also a more secure life.

the country's cities. Nevertheless, the importance of a Jordanian family, whether it lives in a goat hair tent, a one-room cinderblock house, an urban apartment, or an opulent villa, remains a constant. Family honor and welfare continue to be the most precious possessions of the great majority of Jordanians.

One with Arabic Culture

Jordan is part of the unified culture recognized as the Arab world. This means that Jordan shares the attitudes, lifestyles, and cultural heritage of all the countries of the Middle East except Israel. The people of Jordanian territories were part of the Arab world long before the Allied powers created new borders in the Middle East after World War I. The influences of Islam and desert nomadic life and values have given countries of the Arab World a common approach toward literature, art, music, handicrafts, architecture, and food.

This cultural unity supercedes the bitter divisions among neighboring Arab countries. According to Sandra Mackey:

> The Arab world stratifies ethnically, historically, and religiously. It segregates by family and tribe. And it divides by nation. Yet the Arab world is one, joined by the sense of what it means to be Arab. And being Arab means in part drawing identity from an age when the Islamic Empire defined high culture for the world. . . . Islam, which began as a religion in the Arabian Peninsula, became a state governing an empire, and finally a culture that now defines the Arab world.[22]

Islam

More than 90 percent of Jordanians follow Sunni Islam, the majority division of the faith that fundamentally opposes the Shia minority, which rules in Iran. Although Jordanians vary in how strictly they observe the so-called five pillars of Islam, or required acts of worship, they identify with the rest of the Arab world in their overall adherence to the faith. Islam is the state religion. Jordan's 1952 constitution includes a section that requires the king and his successors to be Muslim and the sons of Muslim parents.

Islam means submission to Allah (God), and one who submits is a Muslim. The first of the five pillars is the shahada (testimony) uttered daily by Muslims. It expresses the central belief of Islam: "There is no god but Allah and Muhammad is his prophet."[23]

Salat, or prayer, is the second pillar. Salat gives a structure to Islamic awareness of time and fills the day with a sense of spirituality. It is observed five times daily after ritual washing at dawn, midday, midafternoon, sunset, and nightfall. Worshipers stand facing Mecca, bow repeatedly, and prostrate themselves with foreheads touching the ground. Prayer may be in the form of silently quoting from the sacred text of Islam, the Koran.

The second pillar of Islam, Salat, is observed five times a day. Worshipers face Mecca and prostrate themselves with foreheads touching the ground.

A Muslim house of worship is called a mosque. Although Islam has no ordained clergy, especially learned and respected men may lead prayers or give sermons. When possible, men pray in the mosque and they are expected to do so on Fridays. Women may pray at home or at the mosque, but at the mosque they are segregated from the men.

A muezzin calls the community to prayer.

A Muslim crier, a muezzin, calls the community to prayer at the required times from a minaret, or tower set near the mosque. In modern times, a recording of the haunting call of the muezzin may be broadcast over a loudspeaker. Those out of hearing of the call determine the correct time for prayer using the position of the sun.

The third pillar is zakat, or almsgiving. It used to be a tax imposed by authorities according to a person's wealth and distributed to mosques and the poor. Freewill donations were also given. Now almsgiving is voluntary and usually done through religious foundations known as waqfs.

The fourth pillar is fasting during the holy month of Ramadan, the ninth month of the Muslim calendar. The holiday commemorates Muhammad's receipt of God's revelation, the Koran. It is a month of strict fasting, or avoidance of both food and drink, during daylight hours. The fast applies to all Muslims except the sick, pregnant or nursing women, soldiers on duty, those who must travel, and young children. Some Muslims privately do not observe the fast but will not eat in public at this time.

For those who do possess the needed self-discipline, fasting is an expression of submission to Allah and is also intended to emphasize the equality of all Muslims, strengthening the participants' sense of community. The lunar calendar revolves through solar years, so Ramadan falls in different seasons. Fasting can be especially hard for those who must exert themselves physically in summer; to minimize physical demands, some businesses close for part or all of the day during Ramadan. Each day's fast ends when it is so dark that a black thread cannot be distinguished from a white one. A three-day feast holiday called Id al Fitr concludes Ramadan.

The fifth pillar requires Muslims to undertake a pilgrimage to Mecca, known as the hajj, at least once in a lifetime during the twelfth month of the lunar calendar. The pilgrim dresses in a white garment (ihram) and, upon reaching Mecca, performs ritual ceremonies for several days. Pilgrims then take part in the festival of Eid al Adha, the Festival of Sacrifice, honoring Abraham's obedient decision to sacrifice his son in submission to God's will.

A man who has made the pilgrimage is entitled, when he returns, to the honorific of hajj before his name. A woman who has completed her pilgrimage has earned the title of hajji.

LITERATURE

Islam influences not only the worship, daily life, and holidays of the Arab world, it shapes its followers' creative pursuits as well. Of all creative pursuits, Jordanians, like other Arabs, value literature—poetry, legends, and religious stories—most highly. They cherish the rich literary Arabic of the Koran, considered the model of perfection in Arabic expression. Literary, or classic, Arabic is the language of books, newspapers, magazines, and most radio and television news broadcasts. Although local colloquial dialects dominate ordinary discourse, publication in literary Arabic enables a book or newspaper from any part of the Arab world, such as Iran, to be read and understood by a literate person in any other part, such as Jordan.

Traditional Arabic literature features repetition of short expressions such as phrases and lines and characteristic subject matter. For example, Arab literature frequently deals with love and heroism. A type of Bedouin poetry called qasayed, always begins with a description of the deserted

Mosques

The mosque is an important influence in Islamic architecture; its structure became the basic form of all major Arabic public buildings. The word *mosque* comes from *masjid*, which means "communal prayer." The first mosques in the Arab world were monumental centers of worship meant to show that the revelation given by Allah to Muhammad would last forever. The mosque has historically been used for many purposes: public meetings, sessions of religious courts, shelter for travelers, and hospitals.

Typically, a large mosque is symbolically separated from the rest of the world by an exterior open court. Often worshipers perform ritual ablutions at fountains before prayer. An inner court separates the exterior court and main worship space. Mosque services are conducted facing toward Qiblah, the direction of Mecca; hence the wall on that side is the Qiblah wall. Worshipers arrange themselves in parallel lines, sitting or standing on the floor, but always facing the Qiblah wall. The prayer leader, or imam, stands in a raised niche (mihrab) to the left of a pulpit (nimbar), where he delivers Friday sermons.

Mosques are generally square or rectangular with one large dome and sometimes smaller domes. The walls may be of plaster, Turkish decorated faience (a glazed earthenware or pottery), marble, brick, or stone. Attached to the building, or close by, is the minaret from which the muezzin calls the faithful to prayer.

Jordanian territories were home to some of the earliest mosques in Islam. Magnificent mosques now stand throughout Jordan, including the arresting Abu Darwish Mosque constructed with patterns of black and white stone.

Abu Darwish Mosque, Amman, Jordan.

camping grounds where the poet's beloved once lived and where they were happy together before life separated them.

Poets are greatly respected. Jordan's most cherished classical poet is Mustafa Walibi Al Tal Arar. He was an Arab nationalist, intensely concerned about British and French domination of parts of the Arab world. A social and political activist, he rebelled against governmental and other forms of

authority, once burning contracts peasants had been forced
to sign by landowners. His poem "Al Morabeen" ("The Usu-
rious") reflected his outrage at unfair treatment of the poor.
He also translated several famous literary works, including

MOSAICS

Mosaics are pictures and texts created by pressing ceramic,
glass, or stone fragments into wet plaster. Modern archaeologists exposing
ancient mosaic floors or pavements at Jordanian excavations have revealed
artistic treasures to the world.

Mosaics dating to the first and third centuries have been found in Jerash,
and other Greco-Roman mosaics have been discovered at Machaerus, where
John the Baptist was executed. However, mosaic art reached its peak in the
Byzantine era, from the fall of Rome in 476 to the mid–fourteenth century.
Decorating churches, monasteries, and public buildings, they depict stories,
maps, and writings that often include names and dates of important events.
The ruins of Petra contain a magnificent Byzantine mosaic depicting a per-
sonification of spring.

The undisputed "City of Mosaics" is Madaba, located thirty kilometers
south of Amman. Its riches include the Madaba Map, a sixth-century mosaic
map of Palestine composed of 2 million pieces. Measuring twenty-five by five
meters, the mosaic is located in the Greek Orthodox church of St. George and
was intended to guide pilgrims traveling in the Holy Land. The cities of
Jerusalem, Jericho, and Bethlehem, the River Jordan, the Dead Sea, and Lake
Tiberius appear on the map's surviving fragments.

Hundreds of other mo-
saics are found through-
out Madaba's churches
and homes. Since 1996,
most of the city has been
designated an archeologi-
cal park. Madaba also
boasts the Madaba School
of Mosaic, which teaches
students techniques of
restoring antique mosaics.

*This mosaic adorns the
floor of a sixth-century
church in Jerash, Jordan.*

The Rubáiyát of Omar Khayyám, along with other Persian poetry, into Arabic. Jordanians celebrated the centennial of his birth on May 25, 1999.

Besides the classic themes of love, valor, and religion, Jordanian literature also shares a sense of nationalism with other parts of the Arab world. Beginning in the mid-twentieth century, much literature expresses opposition to foreign interference and the Zionist movement. Two popular Jordanian poets who deal with such themes are a brother and sister, Ibrahim Tuqan and Fawda Tuqan. Literature of recent decades has dealt with Arab-Israeli conflicts, PLO guerrilla actions, and the Palestinian refugees' experiences of loss and hardship.

VISUAL ARTS

Repetition distinguishes Jordanian and other Arabic visual art, as it does the creative arts of literature and music. Repetition is seen in the form of plant, flower, and, most often, geometric motifs, primarily because one interpretation of Islam frowns on representations of living creatures, especially humans, by artists, stressing that only God has the right to fashion them. For that reason, Arabic art tends to move away from nature toward abstract forms. Even a flower might be only suggested by a stemlike curve.

However, some modern painters do include human faces along with other forms in their work. Other visual artists are breaking with the antinatural Arabic visual tradition and openly expressing a connection with the natural world. Khairi Harzallah, a West Bank native now living in Amman, where he sculpts as well as paints, is active in conservation and environmental groups in Jordan. His work shows the influence of Jordan's dramatic landscapes.

The work of such artists is displayed in a growing number of Jordanian galleries. One of these, Darat al Funun, is, according to journalist Ghassan Joha,

> fostering a cultural and creative dialogue among all art lovers in the Arab World. The Darat seeks to strengthen the vitality—and appreciation of—contemporary Arab art, and to help today's visual expressionism take its deserved place as a cornerstone in the building of a contemporary Arab culture.[24]

HANDICRAFTS

Traditional imagery is found not only in the visual arts but also in the ancient practice of Arabic handicrafts. A mix of Arab/Islamic plant, geometric, and sometimes animal patterns found in Jordan and its neighboring countries appears in folk arts whose techniques have been passed down through generations. Part of both livelihood and lifestyle, handicrafts take many forms. Ordinary household objects become significant for their beauty as well as practical uses.

The Bedouin weavers of Jordan and other Arabic countries are the artisans most closely associated with Middle Eastern culture. Bedouin crafters weave sheep's wool and goat and camel hair into many practical items such as bedding bags, rugs, saddlebags, food containers, and room dividers for their tents.

Husband and wife traditionally share the work of preparing to weave. That takes about two months; the wool or hair must be washed, carded, spun, and dyed, and the loom must be set up. Once preparations are complete, the woman does the actual weaving. Other than the natural colors of the animal's coat, traditional Bedouin hues for woven cloth are deep red, black, indigo, green, orange, and mustard, though some color schemes, showing Western influences, include pastels. Jordanian centers of rug making are Al-Karak and Shaubak.

Humble Arabic basketry also continues the tradition of beautiful patterns imposed on practical objects. In Jordan and the rest of the Middle East, designs are woven into the basket using different colors of grass and reeds. Bamboo fronds, split bamboo, and palm leaves are also used to create varieties of trays and baskets. The baskets of former times often had handles because they were used to carry produce to and from the market, or for storing grain. Lidded baskets held laundry.

Embroidery is an old and even more greatly valued craft of Jordanian women. According to custom, village girls learned the art of embroidery knowing that their skill might well affect the quality of husband they would attract. Each Jordanian girl, regardless of her class, embroidered her own trousseau. Intended to last a lifetime, it consisted of from six to twelve loosely cut robes. Although a traditional handicraft, Jordanian embroidery has recently found its way into high fashion designer collections.

Embroidery also has a significant impact on interior decorating because many cushions, and recently quilts, appear in Jordanian homes. Colors include red, maroon, purple, and pink enhanced with green, orange, and gold. The basic cross-stitch forms complicated designs. In keeping with the Arab/Islamic tradition, embroidered cushions display repeated units of trees, flowers, feathers, waves, and geometric forms such as triangles or zigzags.

Like embroidery, jewelry plays an ancient role in Arabic decorative arts. Stores of gold and silver jewelry dating from Roman times have been unearthed at archaeological sites in Jordan. Family wealth was often preserved in the form of jewelry. The Bedouin, often adorned in silver jewelry, might wear bracelets, chokers, rings, hair ornaments, long chains, and rows of coins attached to necklaces or headdresses. Until recent times, a Bedouin bride wore all her wealth as silver jewelry and could do as she pleased with it.

Embroidery is a highly valued craft traditionally taught to every Jordanian girl.

Goldsmiths work outside their shops or bazaar stalls today still using techniques handed down through generations along with the occasional power-driven tool. To create a distinctive appearance, flat surfaces of jewelry may be engraved with Arabic calligraphy.

The art of calligraphy—fine handwriting or script—is valued in all Arabic countries for its beauty and its capacity to enhance Islamic culture. Calligraphy, like geometric and plant designs, allows decoration without the portrayal of human figures. Quotations from the Koran are used to ornament the walls and arches of minarets, mosques, and tombs. They also appear in art and on objects such as jewelry, plates, and embroidered cushions. Lines of poetry also adorn works of decorative art on the facades of buildings. Calligraphy even appears, along with geometric patterns and other pictures, on many Jordanian pickup trucks.

A Jordanian artist who is famous for his masterful calligraphy is the ceramist Mahmoud Taha. He sometimes works with a single letter or combination of letters, not for literal meaning, but for their beauty as abstract forms. However, he, like many other Arab/Islamic artists, still uses calligraphy to depict quotations from the holy Koran in his work.

One handicraft unique to Jordan is the making of sand bottles. For the past several decades, artisans in the regions of Aqaba and Petra have used the naturally occurring colors of area sandstone to fill inexpensive glass bottles with fanciful patterns. A native of Petra, Mohammed Abdullah Othman, taught himself to create these as a child, when he collected his materials from local mountains and caves.

Jordan is proud of all its handicrafts, which also include pottery, blown glass, woodwork, and metalwork. The value of such art lies not only in its cultural heritage, but also as a means of employment for skilled artisans. The Jordanian National Handicraft Project exists to preserve these artists' work and enhance their opportunities for employment. Jordanian folklore and heritage museums in larger cities and universities also celebrate the country's handicrafts.

MUSIC

The repetitive element found in Arabic literature and visual art is also heard in the music of Jordan and the rest of the Arab world. Arab/Islamic music originally served religious purposes, as the Koran was often sung or chanted at prayers, on pilgrimages, or in celebrating the Prophet's birthday. According to Middle East scholar and author Raphael Patai:

> A typical Arab musical piece will begin with one or more instruments playing a brief melodic line, then repeating it several times with or without variation; then the vocalist takes over and does the same; after him, it is again the instruments' turn; then again the vocalist; and so on several times until the conclusion.[25]

Jordanian music is based on a five-tone scale, with twenty-four quarter tones in an octave, instead of the twelve tones in a Western octave. It is sensual, with complicated rhythmic patterns and an absence of the harmonies that appear in Western music. Like all Arab music, Jordanian music tends to be improvisational. A musician, exercising the Arab disregard of time, may step aside from the group and improvise for one or two hours.

Popular instruments include the oud, an instrument with nine to eleven strings the musician plucks; the one-stringed kensansha, an Arabic violin made from a gourd; the flutelike nay; the duff, a tambourine; and the durkakkah, an earthenware drum.

The singer is important and instrumentalists tend to perform mainly as accompanists to singers. (Even in pre-Islamic times in the Middle East, poetry was chanted or sung to instrumental accompaniment.) The status of popular Arabic singers such as delicate-voiced Zamer Bidwan, a graduate of Jordan's National Music Conservatory, is comparable to that of rock stars in the West.

Food

Like folk art and Arabic music passed from generation to generation, traditional Arab cuisine is an important part of Jordanian culture. As a rule, breakfast and supper are light meals, but the midday meal includes hearty dishes. The most frequently served meat is lamb. Islam forbids eating pork, as well as the mixing of meat and milk.

The oud is a popular musical instrument in Jordan.

A popular Jordanian dish for special family occasions and festivals is mansif. Like so many traditions, it originated with the Bedouin. Although goat, camel, or chicken may be used in the dish, most often a sheep is killed, skinned, and cooked. Served with rice, the animal's head is the centerpiece of the dish, topped with a yogurt sauce, chopped parsley, and fried nuts.

Other common Arabic meat dishes popular in Jordan include kofta and kebab. Kofta is spiced ground meat that is skewered and grilled. Kebab is skewered, flame-grilled chunks of meat. Chicken may be used in a kebab instead of lamb. In restaurants, kebabs are often served on parsley with grilled tomatoes and onions. Salads may also accompany a kebab.

Unleavened bread in flat discs about the size of a plate is a staple of the Jordanian diet. Called khobz or khubiz, it is used in place of knives and forks to scoop dips and can also be torn into pieces and used to pick up pieces of meat. A'aish be zaatar, bread seasoned with thyme and other herbs, is also popular. A'aish translates as "life." Bread is never thrown away; uneaten loaves are left out for the poor.

Desserts often come in the form of very sweet pastries, commonly drenched in honey or syrup either alone or in combination with rose water. Other desserts include sweet coconut delicacies and chocolate pudding.

JERASH AND ITS FESTIVAL

Jerash, one of the world's few remaining Greco-Roman outposts, is located only twenty-three miles north of Amman. Known as the Pompeii of the East, Jerash reminds visitors of the grandeur that was Rome. They view the triumphal arch of Hadrian and move to a circle of Corinthian columns at the city center. There, Roman baths and markets as well as cobblestones still carrying marks from chariot wheels are largely preserved.

The restored Greco-Roman amphitheater can seat more than five thousand people. The annual Jerash Festival of Culture and Arts, established through the efforts of Queen Noor and others in 1981, takes place there every July. It is a celebration of Jordanian and many other cultures, and includes troupes of folk dancers, acclaimed ballets, Shakespearien theater, opera, and Arabic comedy. There are poetry readings, concerts, varied competitions, and exhibits of traditional handicrafts such as Bedouin rugs and jewelry. The festival is an embodiment of Jordanian's friendly spirit and love of international cultural richness.

Dark, thick coffee is part of every meal. Usually it is prepared in and poured from a long-handled copper coffee pot into small cups. It frequently carries the scent of cardamom. A guest's cup is promptly refilled unless the guest signals that no more is wanted by tipping the empty cup from side to side. Sweet Bedouin tea is also popular, often served with mint and an ample addition of sugar.

Although Islam also forbids drinking alcohol, some Jordanians do drink beer with side dishes of olives or nuts. In every city, vendors in stalls offer cold fruit beverages that are stored in small clay barrels. These cooling drinks are made of papaya, sugarcane, oranges, lemons, and pineapples.

Along with the abundance of its traditional cuisine, the Arab world is rich in spirituality, language, music, and visual art. Jordan has benefited from and contributed to this richness over centuries. It continues to do so with such internationally known events as the Jerash Festival, as well as in its renewed interest in preserving ancient architecture, handicrafts, and mosaics. It is a country that appreciates beauty and an abundant cultural heritage.

Yet, while cherishing a past rich in beauty and spiritual values, Jordan is mindful of the need for security, well-being, and human rights in the modern world. There are challenges to be met both within and without Jordanian borders.

Bread in the shape of a flat disk and the size of a plate is a staple of the Jordanian diet.

6

CHALLENGES FACING JORDAN TODAY

On February 7, 1999, the day King Hussein died, his eldest son, Abdullah bin al-Hussein, assumed constitutional powers as the monarch of the Hashemite Kingdom of Jordan. The thirty-eight-year-old Abdullah inherited the daunting political, economic, and social challenges facing the kingdom.

Abdullah also had to prove himself as a leader. Many members of the international community expressed doubts about the untried new king's ability. One day after the transfer of power, an editorial in the Swedish newspaper, *Svenska Dagbldet* cautioned:

> Jordan, this small artificial state with many powerful and dangerous neighbors and deep internal opposition, had in King Hussein a monarch who was a skillful statesman. . . . We know little about the political preferences of the newly appointed King Abdullah. The shaping of Jordan's political future therefore is uncertain. But worse is the fact that the state of Jordan—an autocracy lacking democratic institutions—will also in the future be dependent not only on one man's knowledge and interpretation of the surrounding world, but also on his whims.[26]

A more sympathetic assessment comes from a Jordanian palace official: "King Abdullah's challenge is to turn Jordan into a modern state as his predecessor's legacy was to forge a viable nation in the midst of Middle East upheaval."[27]

A year later, King Abdullah himself assessed his leadership role: "This year has really been a sort of crisis management, just to keep people together, to keep them focused and to take a step forward . . . we're still facing many challenges."[28] Within Jordan, two of Abdullah's first challenges are to bring about democratic reforms and to clean up his country's bloated governmental bureaucracy.

FROM SUPPRESSION TO REFORMS

Although Jordan's constitution forbids arrest and imprisonment without due process of law, the declaration of martial law in 1967 introduced emergency regulations that abridged those and other freedoms. Such regulations allowed the secret police of the General Intelligence Department, known as the Mukhabarat, to arrest people suspected of security offenses and hold them, sometimes for many months, without trial or access to their family or legal counsel. The human rights organization Amnesty International has reported that prisoners held by the Mukhabarat have been tortured.

The Mukhabarat was most feared and active during the height of the Palestinian guerrilla activities of the 1970s. It suppressed activities of political parties (all of which were declared illegal), along with expressions of political dissent. It rooted out Palestinian militant groups by keeping an office in every refugee camp. It kept student groups under close observation. It also monitored checkpoints to track domestic travelers and because it authorized issuance of passports, required for both travel and employment, it controlled even study abroad. It often arrested journalists who wrote articles perceived as overly critical or insulting of government officials. Jordanians resented all of these infringements on their human rights.

Just three hours after the death of his father, Prince Abdullah bin al-Hussein is sworn in as the new king of Jordan.

KING ABDULLAH BIN AL-HUSSEIN

Just hours after King Hussein's death on February 7, 1999, his eldest son, Abdullah, assumed constitutional powers as king of Jordan. King Abdullah is the forty-third generation direct descendant of the prophet Muhammad.

King Abdullah was born in Amman on January 30, 1962. Like his father, he received an international education. His early studies were in Jordan at the Islamic Educational College. Secondary education followed at St. Edmund's School in England, then both Eaglebrook School and Deerfield Academy in America.

The king's military education began in 1980 at the Royal Military Academy Sandhurst in the United Kingdom. The Hashemite family has always maintained close ties to Jordan's military. Abdullah began his military career as a captain and commander of a tank company in the 91st Armored Brigade. From 1986 to 1987 he served as a tactics instructor and Cobra attack helicopter pilot in the Royal Jordanian Air Force's helicopter antitank wing. He progressed steadily through the ranks of the armed forces, eventually becoming commander of the Special Operations Command in 1997, and achieved the rank of major general in 1998.

Abdullah also served in the official capacity of regent when King Hussein was out of the country. He traveled widely, sometimes with his father, and sometimes representing Jordan in King Hussein's stead. These official visits enabled him to form bonds with leaders of both the Western and Arab worlds.

King Abdullah married Queen Rania on June 10, 1993. The royal couple has a son, al-Hussein, born June 28, 1994, and a daughter, Princess Iman, born September 27, 1996.

King Abdullah and family.

In 1991 King Hussein took a step toward democratization when he finally ended martial law. In 1992, he took another step by legalizing political parties. The views of some of the resulting political groups, more fundamentalist than the moderate King Hussein would have wished, were not all pleasing to the monarch. However, Jordanians were glad that the king permitted them a greater voice in Jordanian politics.

Since then, hundreds of political prisoners have been released. The restoration of human rights, and increased democratization of Jordanian politics, seems well underway. Abdullah has pledged to continue the path of gradual reform established by his father.

Abdullah's second challenge is to modernize, streamline, and democratize his cumbersome government. By the late 1980s, increasingly dissatisfied Jordanians were openly criticizing government bureaucracy and corruption. This corruption derived from tribal nepotism (awarding jobs to family) and a long-standing system of political patronage (giving jobs in exchange for political favors). Middle East scholar Helen Chapin Metz observes, "Members of the middle class particularly seemed to have gained an awareness that the liberties they enjoyed were based primarily on the king's benevolence rather than on . . . democratic rights and a system of checks and balances on . . . centralized authority."[29]

Those close to King Abdullah say he believes that Jordan's future stability depends on political reforms and free market policies that steer the country away from tribally based nepotism toward modern statehood. The patronage system is deeply entrenched, however, and 43 percent of the national budget goes to public sector salaries. Not surprisingly, the king has met heavy resistance to reform from the old government bureaucracy. This establishment feeds popular fears that the king's reforms, focusing on privatization and deregulation, carry social and political risks. Changing such a deeply rooted system will not be an easy or rapid task.

Still, King Abdullah has won praise from many of his subjects by visiting government departments and state hospitals in disguise to assess their efficiency and the courtesy of their staffs. He targets agencies where aides have reported serious problems. After standing in lines and receiving treatment as an ordinary citizen, he files an official report. If improvements are not evident, the inefficient civil servants are replaced. While disguised, perhaps as an old Arab man, he also visits with Jordanians on the street to see what they think of the administration. "After my first visits it was sort of like Elvis," he is quoted as saying. "There were sightings all over the country."[30]

RENEWING FRIENDSHIPS

Turning to foreign relations, King Abdullah realized that another challenge would be to mend Jordan's bonds with other

Arab countries. Some were severed by Arab neighbors who condemned Jordan's siding with Iraq during the Gulf War. Jordan had further compromised its solidarity with its Arab neighbors when King Hussein signed a peace agreement with Israel in 1994.

Meeting the problem of Arab world disapproval head on, King Abdullah renewed diplomatic relations with Syria, Kuwait, and Saudi Arabia during his first weeks in power. He pledged never to pursue relations with Israel at the cost of relations with Arab countries, saying publicly, "With the new reign, we are opening a clean sheet with everyone based on mutual respect. Jordan is Arab first and last and cannot shed its skin."[31]

Even though King Abdullah appears to favor relations with Arab neighbors over a friendship with Israel, he seeks peace in the Middle East, which necessarily entails Jordanian/Israeli diplomatic negotiations. Abdullah must handle conflicts with Israel concerning trade, water rights, and his own determination to consolidate Jerusalem's Islamic holy sites, such as the Al Aqsa Mosque, under Jordanian control.

King Abdullah is also working to forge diplomatic relations with PLO leaders. The question of a Palestinian state continues. Abdullah, like his father, does not wish to see Jordan become the official Palestinian homeland, which would likely pose a challenge to the strength and perhaps even continued existence of the Hashemite monarchy. Palestinians in Jordan outnumber the Jordanian Arabs, and it is the Jordanian Arabs, especially the Bedouin, who have traditionally been most loyal to their Hashemite kings.

THE ECONOMY

King Abdullah's efforts to gain and maintain success as a monarch are linked to his country's economic progress and his people's sense of economic security. Jordan's economy has always been a mixture of government-owned or -sponsored business and private enterprise. For decades the government has been the sole channel through which foreign aid, loans, and expatriate workers' wages are funneled. The government distributes these funds to the private sector and therefore acts as a financier. The government has also adopted companies that the private sector did not have funds to start, and has taken over certain banks or export companies when they could not produce a profit.

Governmental bureaucracy has therefore been seen as a sort of deep pocket by Jordanians. Used to the security of government subsidies, Jordanians have not been as eager to risk investing in private business and production as the government would like.

Still, definite changes are taking place. For example, the government is acting to privatize the formerly state-owned telecommunications industry. King Abdullah has sought to enact reforms through his position as chair of an economic advisory council made up of a nongovernmental entrepreneurial elite that advocates Western business methods. The council's goal is to create a dynamic, investor-friendly environment that will be enhanced by government policies. He has found that he must move with caution, however. Many Jordanians dependent on the state fear that shrinking governmental involvement in commerce will expose them to the risks and unpredictability that are part of a free market.

King Abdullah's fence-mending with other Middle Eastern countries has boosted Jordan's economy, but besides the problems of developing a healthy free market, the country has suffered economic setbacks since the Persian Gulf War. Tourism fell off; Jordan struggled under enormous international debt from foreign aid; development aid from the disapproving West and other Arab countries evaporated; and an

During his first year as king, Abdullah worked hard to mend fences and forge stronger relations with Jordan's Arab neighbors such as Palestinian leader Yasir Arafat.

influx of refugees and of returning Jordanians who had been employed in neighboring countries' oil fields increased Jordan's already high rate of unemployment and need for social services. But thanks to Abdullah's diplomatic approach during his initial reign, a friendlier Saudi Arabia and other oil states transferred money to Jordan to strengthen the dinar, Jordan's currency, which had declined in value.

King Abdullah has also appealed to the West to help Jordan deal with its $7 billion debt. During a six-nation Western tour he asked American president Bill Clinton to help convince the world's leading industrial nations to forgive half the amount owed. He also continues the reform programs started by his father to restructure remaining debt. Jordan has always depended on external aid, and debt remains an ongoing problem as it has from the country's inception.

AGRICULTURE AND WATER

Jordan's economy suffers in large part because the country is poor in natural resources, and the most sharply felt is the lack of water. Twenty percent of the population farms and raises livestock, mainly sheep, goats, camels, and poultry. The fortunate farmers are those in the Jordan River Valley, blessed with an extensive irrigation system and a subtropical climate suitable for growing fruits and vegetables. Farmers increase production through use of greenhouses, drip irrigation, improved seed strains, inorganic fertilizers, and mechanization.

But much of Jordan's agriculture is pursued in dry areas that suffer long, periodic droughts. Although research is being conducted to find drought-resistant crops, such as new strains of grains and potatoes, the droughts can be devastating.

Abdullah continues the work begun by his father in addressing this problem. Exploration for groundwater and research into desalinization of water from the Red Sea for irrigation is in progress. In part one of an agreement reached between Syria and Jordan in May 1999, Syria agreed to pump water into Jordan, parched from a severe regional drought.

The rest of the three-part agreement concerned cooperation between the countries in the production of electricity and the exploitation of mineral wealth. It calls for joint marketing of agricultural products, a joint dam, a bilateral electric link project, and cooperation in oil and natural gas exploration.

Plants such as this one extract potash from the Dead Sea and process it into potassium chloride.

MINING AND INDUSTRY

Such exploration is important because discovery of oil deposits and natural gas reserves would change Jordan's status as the poor relation in the Arab family of countries. There is one oil field near Iraq and some natural gas reserves have been found at al-Rishah. Jordan's one oil refinery at Zarqa handles Jordan's oil production as well as crude oil imported from neighboring countries. Oil shale may prove to be an asset through the process of extracting oil by distillation from the rock.

Although Jordan sponsors oil and natural gas exploration, its only proven mineral resources are phosphate and potash, both used in fertilizer. Jordan has from 1.5 billion to 2.5 billion tons of phosphate reserves. That means Jordan can continue to produce phosphate for export for centuries. Presently, the export of prosphate brings in about 20 percent of Jordan's export revenue.

Potash is now being extracted by means of solar energy from the Dead Sea. The Arab Potash Company processes the potash into potassium chloride. India is among its major customers. Recently, Finnish interests have announced a plan to invest heavily in Jordanian potash extraction.

King Abdullah's government has shown its serious intent to promote mining and chemical processing by becoming a party to the European Free Trade Agreement (EFTA). This led Nork Hydro, Norway's biggest industrial conglomerate, to plan an investment of over $700 million in a joint venture with the Jordan Phosphate Mines Company to develop fertilizer production. In May 1999, the European Investment Bank (EIB) approved a loan of 30 million Euro ($ 25,518,00) to the Jordan Phosphate Mines Company for expanded phosphate mining in southern Jordan, expected to increase national production capacity by 36 percent.

The downside of this industrial development is that, according to studies by the Jordanian Society for Sustainable Development, the mineral extraction is by open mines, creating air and water pollution and health hazards to workers. Mining also presents a drain on Jordan's scant freshwater resources.

ENVIRONMENTAL ISSUES

Mining's effect on the environment is being monitored as part of a growing concern for Jordan's ecology. Although Jordan has a variety of beautiful terrain and wildlife, the environment has suffered greatly from overgrazing and other abuses. Current issues include limited natural freshwater resources and deforestation, which has brought on desertification, the process by which arable land turns to desert.

Such problems face other countries in the Middle East; the increasing competition for life-sustaining water and fertile land has fueled discord in the region. In her address to the 1998 forum of the International Union for the Conservation of Nature and Natural Resources, Jordanian Queen Noor explained, "We are caught in a vicious cycle: comprehensive solutions . . . will arise only through comprehensive peace, but the scarcity of resources such as water and arable land is one of the sources of conflict. It is important to see the environment not as a luxury to be attended to after peace has been achieved, but as a key issue for regional stability."[32]

The problems are serious, but Jordan is making determined efforts to confront them, beginning in the 1960s with the founding of the first environmental society in the Arab World, the Royal Society for the Conservation of Nature. Six nature reserves have been established in Jordan and plans exist for six more. There are numerous environmental groups

THE SHAUMARI WILDLIFE RESERVE

Jordan's Royal Society for the Conservation of Nature is a government-sponsored organization charged with creating a network of protected lands. The first tract so designated, Shaumari, was created in 1975 in the semiarid northeastern region of Badia bordering Syria.

The Shaumari reserve, occupying about eight and a half square miles, was established for the special purpose of protecting an endangered desert antelope, the Arabian oryx. Sometimes called the white oryx, this animal is said to have inspired the legend of the unicorn. The Arabian oryx had been hunted to extinction in Jordan by the 1930s. In an international rescue effort in 1978, eight animals were flown to Jordan from the Phoenix Zoo in Arizona. By 1999, the Jordanian herd numbered over two hundred.

Similar projects at Shaumari include breeding programs for other endangered or locally extinct desert animals, including the Persian onager, a relative of the extinct wild ass; the ostrich; and the goitered gazelle.

Observation towers allow visitors to view these rare creatures. During spring and autumn many migrating birds rest here at the only freshwater spring-fed pools in the surrounding twelve thousand square miles of desert. Other wild creatures that can be seen are the Cape hare, red fox, gerbil, striped hyena, and wild cat.

The near-extinct Arabian oryx is thought to have inspired the legend of the unicorn.

such as the Jordanian Society for Desertification Control and Badia Development, which transforms barren land into national parks. The Jordan Environment Society is dedicated to environmental education and fighting air pollution, and the Jordan Royal Ecological Diving Society protects Aqaba's marine life and coral reefs. Efforts to save endangered species such as the Arabian oryx (a kind of antelope) have intensified.

TOURISM

Jordan's natural beauty is a vital asset in the promotion of tourism by both the royal family and the Ministry of Tourism and Antiquities. The tourism industry suffered a severe blow

Jordan promotes its historical sites such as the Roman amphitheater at Jerash to help increase tourism.

with the 1967 loss of the West Bank, which included Jerusalem, Bethlehem, Nablus, and Jericho. Today, however, tourism, one of Jordan's fastest growing industries, is expected to thrive as long as peace exists. Even without the West Bank, Jordan has not only natural, but historic, religious, and cultural resources to lure international visitors, and its population is known to be one in the most friendly and tolerant in the Middle East.

The Ministry of Tourism and Antiquities promotes historic sites such as the Roman amphitheater of Jerash, the Nabatean ruins of Petra, and the great desert region of Wadi Rum. There visitors can ride horses or camels, camp, rock climb, or float in hot air balloons. Potential additions to the tourism infrastructure include a proposal to locate "The Lowest Park on Earth" at the Dead Sea.

The growing profits generated by the tourism sector are clearly linked to peace, as well as to the ministry's efforts. The 1994 peace agreement between Jordan and Israel showed immediate results when, by mid-1995, over twenty thousand Israelis had flocked to Jordan's five-star hotels and tourist attractions. Jordan, Israel, and Egypt are even considering a joint project with resort facilities to be known as the Red Sea Riviera. Tourism growth should continue provided there is peace and investment from both the government and the private sector.

POPULATION CONCERNS

A final concern for Jordan as the country enters the twenty-first century is potential overpopulation. Jordan's 2.6 percent birth rate is one of the highest on earth: At this rate the nation's population of 4.7 million could double by 2026. Because 30 percent of the people of this resource-poor country already live below the poverty line, such an increase in population could overwhelm social services and outpace employment. The government is focusing on family planning policies that include making contraceptives available to Jordanians through clinics and pharmacies. The Ministry of Health is also using television and radio to provide information to the public concerning reproductive issues.

Jordan remains a country rich in history and tradition, but one which must meet many challenges. Poverty, over population, and a scarcity of natural resources all threaten the welfare of its people. The last king in the world to rule by divine right, King Abdullah must bring his country into the twenty-first century by furthering progress toward economic well-being and democratization. In addition, he must build on his father's legacy of working for tolerance and peace in the Middle East. He will have plenty of help in these endeavors; a turbulent past has left Jordanians eager for peace and a voice in their own destiny.

FACTS ABOUT JORDAN

GOVERNMENT

Full Name: Hashemite Kingdom of Jordan

Independence: May 25, 1946 (from League of Nations mandate under British administration); May 25 is now a national holiday.

Type: A hereditary, constitutional monarchy based on the constitution of 1952.

Executive Branch: King Abdullah II has been chief of state since February 7, 1999. His appointed prime minister is head of government. The cabinet is appointed by the prime minister in consultation with the monarch.

Legislative Branch: The bicameral National Assembly consists of the Senate (a forty-member body appointed by the king from categories of public figures; members serve four-year terms) and the House of Representatives (eighty seats; members are elected by popular vote on the basis of proportional representation to serve four-year terms).

Judicial Branch: The legal system derives from a mixture of Islamic law and French, British, and Ottoman systems. There are no juries. In order of importance the courts are: the Court of Cassation; the Courts of Appeal; the Courts of First Instance; the Magistrates' Courts; and Religious Courts.

Political Parties: Political parties have been legal since 1992. They include the Jordanian National Alliance; Popular Unity Party; Jordanian Pledge Party; Unionist Arab Democratic Party; Homeland Party; Islamic Action Front; Arab Islamic Democratic Movement; and pan-Arab Nationalist, Baathist, and Communist Parties.

Capital: Amman

Administrative divisions: 12 governorates: Ajlun, Al'Aqabah, Al Balqa', Al Karak, Al Mafraq, 'Amman, At Tafiliah, Az Zarqa', Irbid, Jarash, Ma'an, Madaba.

Flag: The flag is a tricolor with equal horizontal bands from top to bottom of black, white, and green with a red isosceles triangle on the hoist side bearing a seven-pointed white star; the seven points on the star represent the seven fundamental laws of the Koran.

National Anthem: "Asha al Malik" ("Long Live the King")

Religion: Islam (about 96% of Jordanians are Sunni Muslim, about 4% Christian; about half of the Christians are Greek Orthodox).

Languages: Arabic is the official language; English is spoken widely among middle and upper classes.

PEOPLE

Population: 4,561,147 (July 1999 est.)

Population growth rate: 3.05%

Birth rate: 34.31 births/1,000 population

Infant mortality rate: 32.7 deaths/1,000 live births

Life expectancy at birth:

Total population: 73.06 years

Male: 71.15 years

Female: 75.08 years

Ethnic Groups: Arab 98%; Circassian 1%, Armenian 1%. A majority of the Arab population is referred to as Palestinian; a Palestinian was originally a citizen of the British-mandated territory of Palestine (1922–1948). Generally now it means a Muslim or Christian native or descendant of a native of the area between the Egyptian Sinai and Lebanon and west of the Jordan River–Dead Sea–Gulf of Aqaba line who identifies himself or herself as a Palestinian.

Literacy:

Total population: 86.6%

Male: 93.4%

Female: 79.4%

Communication:

Four daily newspapers and twenty-two weeklies. The *Jordan Times* is published in English. Newspapers were denationalized in 1990. There is no prepublication censorship, but the government may confiscate publications that prove disturbing in areas of religion, morality, national dignity, or public order.

There are 425,000 telephones (1998 est.).

There are 1.1 million radios.

There are 350,000 televisions.

There are approximately 35 cinemas.

GEOGRAPHY

Land Area: 37,738 square miles, a bit smaller than Indiana. From north to south, the greatest distance is 230 miles; from east to west, 230 miles. Jordan has 16 miles of coastline.

Border Countries: Syria on the north, Iraq on the northeast, Saudi Arabia on the east and south, Israel and the West Bank on the west.

Highest Point: Jabal Rum, 5,755 ft.

Lowest point: Shore of the Dead Sea, about 1,300 ft. below sea level.

Terrain: Jordan's terrain is mostly desert plateau in the east and highland area in the west; the Great Rift Valley separates East and West Banks of the Jordan River.

Rivers: The Jordan River is 97 miles long and empties into the Dead Sea. Its largest tributary is the Yarmouk River. The Nahr az-Zarqa flows across the eastern plateau north of Amman.

Land Use:

    Arable land: 4%

    Permanent crops: 1%

    Permanent pastures: 9%

    Forests and woodland: 1%

    Other: 85%

Environmental issues: limited natural freshwater resources; deforestation; overgrazing; soil erosion; desertification.

CLIMATE

Jordan has an arid Mediterranian climate with hot dry summers and cool wet winters, although the highlands may have cooler summers and cold winters. There is a rainy season from November to April in the west. The Jordan River Valley has an average rainfall of eight inches. Average monthly temperatures in Amman range from 44 to 87 degrees F.; temperatures in the south range from 61 to 90 degrees F. During the summer, khamsin—hot, dusty winds— blow from the southeast.

ECONOMY

Monetary Unit: Jordanian dinar (JD)

Gross Domestic Product: (1995) $6.5 billion. Jordan's lack of natural resources results in its having one of the smallest economies in the Arab world. Agriculture contributes 6% to the economy; industry, 30%; and services 64%.

Annual per capita income: $3,500.

Unemployment rate: 15% plus

Exports: Approximately $1.5 billion: commodities are phosphates, fertilizers, potash, agricultural products, manufactured goods such as pharmaceuticals, textiles, cement, plastics, detergent, and soap.

Imports: Approximately $3.9 billion: commodities include crude oil, machinery, transport equipment, food, live animals, and manufactured goods.

Major trading partners: Exports mainly to India, Saudi Arabia, Iraq, Indonesia, and United Arab Emirates. Imports mainly from the United States, Germany, Japan, Italy, United Kingdom, and Turkey.

ARMED FORCES

Military Branches: Jordanian Armed Forces (JAF includes Royal Jordanian Land Force, Royal Naval Force, and Royal Jordanian Air Force); Badiya (irregular) Border Guards; Ministry of the Interior's Public Security Force (under JAF only in wartime or crises).

NOTES

CHAPTER 1: GEOGRAPHY AND EARLY HISTORY

1. Robert St. John, *Roll Jordan Roll: The Life Story of a River and Its People*. Garden City, NY: Doubleday, 1965, pp. 78–79.

2. Quoted in St. John, *Roll Jordan Roll*, p. 394.

3. St. John, *Roll Jordan Roll*, p. 213.

4. St. John, *Roll Jordan Roll*, pp. 369–70.

CHAPTER 2: THE FORMATION OF MODERN JORDAN

5. Sandra Mackey, *Passion and Politics: The Turbulent World of the Arabs*. New York: Dutton, 1992, p. 83.

6. Quoted in Mackey, *Passion and Politics*, p. 104.

7. Mackey, *Passion and Politics*, pp. 104–105.

8. Helen Chapin Metz, ed., *Jordan: A Country Study*. Washington, DC: Federal Research Division, Library of Congress, 1991, p. 26.

9. Mackey, *Passion and Politics*, p. 192.

CHAPTER 3: THE MODERATE MONARCH

10. Metz, *Jordan*, p. xxi.

11. Mackey, *Passion and Politics*, p. 198.

12. Quoted in Mackey, *Passion and Politics*, p. 201.

13. Quoted in Mackey, *Passion and Politics*, p. 209.

14. Milton Viorst, "Jordan: A Moderate's Role," wysiwyg:// 22/www.theatlantic.com/issues/81mar/hussein.htm, p. 8.

CHAPTER 4: DAILY LIFE

15. Metz, *Jordan*, p. 93.

16. Michael Beard, Ph.D., telephone interview with author, August 12, 2000.

17. Viorst, "Jordan, a Moderate's Role," p. 1.

18. Milton Viorst, *Sandcastles: The Arabs in Search of the Modern World.* New York: Knopf, 1994, p. 301.

19. Metz, *Jordan*, p. 82.

20. Mackey, *Passion and Politics*, pp. 29–30.

21. Mackey, *Passion and Politics*, p. 13.

CHAPTER 5: ONE WITH ARAB CULTURE

22. Mackey, *Passion and Politics*, p. 41.

23. Quoted in Metz, *Jordan*, p. 106.

24. Ghassan Joha, "Darat al Funun: Summer Festival brightens up Amman," at http://star.arabia.com/980827/Fel.html, p. 1.

25. Raphael Patai, *The Arab Mind.* New York: Charles Scribners Sons, 1973, p. 170.

CHAPTER 6: CHALLENGES FACING JORDAN TODAY

26. Gail Hamer Burke, ed., February 8, 1999, "King Hussein Dies: Jordan's Torch Is Passed; 'Huge Loss' to ME Peace," at http://www.usia.gov/admin/005/wwwh9f08.html, p. 8.

27. Quoted in "King Abdullah Faces Daunting Challenges," Arabia on Line, February 8, 2000, at http://arabia.com/article/0,1690,News-12931,00.html, pp. 11–12.

28. Quoted in "King Abdullah," Arabia on Line, p. 1.

29. Metz, *Jordan*, p. xxviii-xxvix.

30. "King Abdulla," Arabia on Line, p. 3.

31. Quoted in Andra Brack, Weekend News Today, Dateline Israel, April 12, 1999, "King Abdullah of Jordan," at www.arabia.com/content/news/599/lahoud29.shtml;http://philolgos.org/bpr/Files/misc-Sstudies/ms045.htm, p. 7.

32. Her Majesty Queen Noor, Address to the International Union for the Conservation of Nature and Natural Resources (IUCN), Regional Forum in Amman. 10 February, 1998, at www.noor.gov.jo/main/iucnamm.htm, p. 7.

CHRONOLOGY

B.C.

2000
Semitic people arrive in the Jordan River Valley.

732
Jordanian territories conquered by Assyrians.

587
Babylonians conquer Jordanian territories.

198
Greek rule of the Seleucids in Jordanian territories.

63
Rome dominates Jordanian territories.

A.D.

633
Islamic Arab armies from Saudi Arabia invade Jordanian territories and Syria.

1099
Knights of the First Crusade seize Jordanian lands.

1187
Saladin defeats the crusaders and founds the Ayyubid dynasty.

1250
The Mameluks invade from Egypt and establish rule.

1517
Ottoman Turks defeat the Mameluks and rule until the British-backed Arab revolt.

1916
Sharif Hussein ibn Ali leads Arab nationalists in their revolt against the Ottomans.

1920
Britain receives a mandate for Palestine and Transjordan.

1921
Abdullah ibn Hussein becomes the ruler of Transjordan.

1946
Britain recognizes Transjordan as an independent sovereign state with Abdullah as its monarch.

1947
The UN General Assembly votes to partition Palestine into Jewish and Arab states. Arabs protest.

1948
State of Israel is established. Five Arab League states, including Jordan, attack Israel.

1949
Transjordan becomes the Hashemite Kingdom of Jordan. Jordan annexes the West Bank and refugees stream into Jordan.

1951
Abdullah is assassinated. Talal becomes king.

1953
Hussein becomes king.

1955
Jordan joins the United Nations.

1959
Jordan offers citizenship to all Palestinian refugees.

1967
Jordan signs mutual defense pact with Egypt. Six Day War. Israel attacks Egypt, Jordan, and Syria and captures the West Bank, among other lands.

1970–1971
Jordanian Civil War. King Hussein defeats Palestinian guerrillas. Palestine Liberation Organization (PLO) withdraws its headquarters from Jordan.

1974
Arab Summit Conference recognizes PLO as sole representative of Palestinian interests.

1978
Jordan, along with most Arab states, the PLO, and the Soviet Union, rejects the Camp David Accords signed by U.S.

president Jimmy Carter, Egyptian president Anwar Sadat, and Israeli prime minister Menachem Begin.

1986

King Hussein begins development programs to strengthen his position in the West Bank.

1988

Hussein gives up legal claims and administrative ties to the West Bank; advocates creation of a Palestinian state to be governed by the PLO.

1990–1991

Jordan sides with Iraq in the Gulf War.

1994

A peace agreement with Israel signed on October 26 ends forty-six years of hostilities.

1999

King Hussein dies February 7. His eldest son, Abdullah, becomes king.

SUGGESTIONS FOR FURTHER READING

William Dudley, ed., *The Middle East*. San Diego: Greenhaven Press, 1992. Anthology of opposing viewpoints on Middle East issues.

Leila Merrill Foster, *Jordan: The Enchantment of the World*. Chicago: Childrens Press, 1991. An overview of Jordan including history, tourist sites, and culture.

Arthur Goldschmidt Jr., *A Concise History of the Middle East*. Boulder, CO: Westview Press, 1979. A study of Islamic culture, Western influence, and the struggles for Arab independence and the Arab/Israeli conflict.

James Haskins, *Leaders of the Middle East*. Hillside, NJ: Enslow, 1985. Relates Middle Eastern history through biographies of nine of its major leaders.

Edward Jablonski, *A Pictorial History of the Middle East: War and Peace from Antiquity to the Present*. Garden City, NY: Doubleday, 1986. A panoramic look at conflicts in the Middle East from the Crusades to recent times.

Lerner Publications, Geography Department, *Jordan in Pictures*. Minneapolis: Lerner, 1988. Text and photographs introduce the geography, history, government, people, and economy of Jordan.

Peter Mansfield, *The Arab World: A Comprehensive History*. New York: Thomas Y. Crowell, 1976. On the foundation of a general history of the Arab world, the author studies individual Arab nations, and economic and political issues.

Antony Mason, *Middle East*. Englewood Cliffs, NJ: Silver Burdett, 1988. People and Places Series. A look at the geography, climate, industry, culture, history, environment, and wildlife of the Middle East.

François Massoulié, *Middle East Conflicts*. Brooklyn: Inter-link Books, 1999. The author, a French scholar-diplomat, analyzes the conflicts of the Middle East with an objective look at its history.

WORKS CONSULTED

BOOKS

George Antonius, *The Arab Awakening: The Story of the Arab National Movement*. New York: Capricorn Books, 1965. A full account of the Arab national movement.

Jacques Berque, *The Arabs: Their History and Future*. Trans. Jean Stewart. New York: Praeger, 1965. A study of the Arab world since WWII based on the author's personal experience and on Arab studies and journals.

Jimmy Carter, *The Blood of Abraham: Insights into the Middle East*. Boston: Houghton Mifflin, 1985. The former president presents explanations of each Middle East nation's interpretation of the religious issues that have led to centuries of conflict in the Arab world.

Albert Hourani, *A History of the Arab Peoples*. Cambridge, MA: Belknap Press of Harvard University Press, 1991. A comprehensive coverage of Arab history and contemporary issues such as the Palestine question and the role of women.

Lloyd Kahn, ed., *Shelter*. Bolinas, CA: Shelter Publications, 1973. An informative collection of writings about the construction of dwelling places around the world.

David Lamb, *The Arabs: Journeys Beyond the Mirage*. New York: Random House, 1987. An overview of the Arab world that considers its achievements and dilemmas.

Bernard Lewis, *The Middle East: A Brief History of the Last 2,000 Years*. New York: Scribner, 1995. A scholarly and readable history of the forces that shaped the Middle East.

Sandra Mackey, *Passion and Politics: The Turbulent World of the Arabs*. New York: Dutton, 1992. A lively chronicle of the Arab world that explores of the bonds holding it together as well as its rivalries.

Helen Chapin Metz, ed., *Jordan: A Country Study*. Washington, DC: Federal Research Division, Library of Congress,

1991. A portrayal of political, economic, social, and national security systems and institutions and how they shape Jordan's culture.

Alan Murphy and Justin Flynn, coordinators. *Lonely Planet: the Middle East.* 3rd ed. Melbourne: Lonely Planet Publications, 2000. An informative guide for the independent traveler.

Raphael Patai, *The Arab Mind.* New York: Charles Scribner's Sons, 1973. Beginning with the typical upbringing of an Arab child, the author examines the traditions of Arab society and their effect on Arabs' social and political behavior.

Francis Robinson, ed., *The Cambridge Illustrated History of the Islamic World.* New York. Cambridge University Press, 1996. A study of the Muslim world from the eighth to the eighteenth centuries, including the economy, social order, and art, and the Islamic culture's connections to the West.

Robert St. John, *Roll Jordan Roll: The Life Story of a River and Its People.* Garden City, NY: Doubleday, 1965. A history of the Jordan River Valley and its residents to the modern age.

Editors of Time-Life Books, *What Life was Like in the Lands of the Prophet: Islamic World AD 570 1405.* Alexandria, VA: Time-Life Books, 1999. One of a series on world history that uses art, artifacts, and personal accounts to depict daily life in the past.

Barry Turner, ed., *The Statesman's Yearbook: The Politics, Cultures, and Economies of the World.* New York: St. Martin's, 2000. Current facts about Jordan.

Milton Viorst, *Sandcastles: The Arabs in Search of the Modern World.* New York: Knopf, 1994. A look at seven key Arab countries, including discussion of how Jordan's monarchy coexists with democracy.

INTERNET SOURCES

Raed Al Abed, "Lack of awareness and dull campaign tactics behind women failure to reach the dome," http://star.arabia.com/971113/J03.html.

"Aqaba, Gulf of," Article from Encyclopedia Britannica. wysiwyg//34//http://www.britannica.com/bcom/eb/article/idxref/1/0,5716,307119,00.html.

Koffi Attah, "Calligraphy on crafts unveils Jordan's treasure haven," http://star.arabia.com/981022/FE1.html.

——— , "Oriental gift shops of Amman carry onlooker to another age," http://star.arabia.com/970814/J04.html.

"Basic Country Facts," 1997, www.arabicnews.com/Basic Facts/JORDAN/people.html.

Chris Bradley, "Jordan, A Look at Wildlife Reserves," www.arabianwildlife.com/past-arw/vol2.2/jor.htm.

Gail Hamar Burke, ed., February 8, 1999, "King Hussein Dies: Jordan's Torch Is Passed, 'Huge Loss' to ME Peace," http://www.usia.gov/admin/005/wwwh9f08.html.

Francesca Ciriaci, "Opposition, independents send 'natural plan' for reform to King," www.jordanembassyus.org/022899004.htm.

"Country Profile: Hashemite Kingdom of Jordan," www.awo.net/country/overview/crjor.asp.

"Culture," www.arab.net/jordan/culture/jn_basketry.html.

www.arab.net/jordan/culture/jn__ceramics.html.

www.arab.net/jordan/culture/jn_embroidery.html.

www.arab.net/jordan/culture/jn_food.html.

www.arab.net/jordan/culture/jn_glass.html.

www.arab.net/jordan/culture/jn_jewellry.html.

www.arab.net/jordan/culture/jn_weaving.html.

"Culture, 'Handicrafts,' 'Cuisine,'" www.mota.gov.jo/CAT5-o6.HTM

"Destination Jordan," www.lonelyplanet.com/dest/mea/jor.htm.

Encyclopedia Britannica: "Jordan, Cultural Life, Daily Life," wysiwyg//10/http://www.britannica.com/bcom/eb/article/3/0,5716,109573+l+106459,00.html.

Munther Hamdan, "Feature: Reflecting the modern history of the region: Railways with the past." "The ancient Art of Mosaics: Detailing Jordan's History," http://corp.arabia.com/JordanToday/index/feature.htm.

"Islamic Architecture," www.islamicart.com/main/architecture /intro.htm.

Abu Jafar, M.Z., and C. Hays-Shahin, "Reintroduction of the Arabian Oryx into Jordan." in A. Doxon and D. Jones, eds., *Conservation and biology of desert antelopes.* London: Christopher Helm Ltd., 1988, Abstract. http://mercury.bio. uaf.edu/-bgriffit.faculty/mammals.html.

Ghassan Joha, "Darat al Funan: Summer Festival brightens up Amman." August, 27 1998. http://star.arabia.com/980827/ Fel.html.

Rama Husseini, "Former deputy Faisal aims to blaze trail for women in 2001 elections," www.middleeastwire.com/ jordan/stories/2000811_7_meno.shtml.

Jani's Excursion to the Hashemite Kingdom of Jordan. Day 2:Kerak, Petra. http://jpatokal.iki.fi/text/jordan/day2.html.

Jewish Student Online Research Center (JSOURCE) for the American-Israeli Cooperative Enterprise, "King Abdullah bin al-Hussein." http://www.us-israel/org/jsource/biography/ Abdullah.html.

"Jordan to Host Global Summit on Peace through Tourism November 8–10, 2000, In Amman," www.iipt.org/inthe news/jordan.html.

Jordan Tourism Board—Places in Time—Archeological Sites. www.tourism.com.jo/places-in-time/bottom_archeological. html.

"Jordan's Archeological Heritage." www.noor.gov.jo?main /cjah.htm.

"Jordanians protest 'honor crimes,'" http://detnews.com:80 /2000/religion/0002/20/02150012.htm.

Zerhan Karabiber, "Acoustical Problems in Mosques," ASA?EAA/DAGA '99. www.acoustics.org/137th/karabiber. html.

Lubna Khader, "Jordanian poet Mustafa Wahbi Al Tal in Memory of time," http://star.arabia.com/990513/FE3. html.

Tore Kjeilen, "Gulf of Aqaba," *Encyclopaedia of the Orient.* wysiwyg://read.6/http://i-cias.com/e.o/aqaba-gl.htm.

"King Abdullah of Jordan." Submitted by research-bpr@philologos.org for Bible Prophecy research. http://philologos.org/bpr/files/Misc_Studies/ms045.htm.

"King Abdullah Faces Daunting Challenges," http://arabia.com/article/0,1690,News.12931,00.html.

"King Abdullah bin Al-Hussein (1882–1951)," www.kinghussein.gov.jo/kingabdullah.htm.

Oystein S. LaBianca, "Indigenous hardiness structures and state formation in Jordan," www.hf.uib.no/smi/paj/LaBianca.html.

Nelly Lama, Darat al Funun news & press clips: "Pioneers of Jordan: Mahmoud Taha, Ceramist, Exhibits at Darat El Funun," www.daratalfunun.org/main/acitivit/presscl/taha.html.

"T. E. Lawrence (Lawrence of Arabia) English Soldier and author," www.lucidcafe.com/library/95aug./lawrence.html.

Rasha Lasawi and Rania Wakileh, "Interview by the Magazine Al-Shouman of the National School for Girls. Jordan Artist Interview of the Arab Artist Nawaf Al-Bukhari of Amman, Jordan," www.gallery offineart.com/AutoBio/Pages/ShoumE.html.

"Mosaics and the Madabga School of the Byzantine Period," www.imarabe.org/all/temp/expo/jordanie-us/jordanie5.html.

"Nature Reserves. Shaumari," www.rscn.org.jo/wildjo 2.html.

"H. M. Queen Noor of Jordan," August 16, 1999. The Hashemite Royal Court of Jordan, www.noor.gov.jo?main/resume.htm.

"Queen Noor's Address to the IUCN Regional Forum in Amman, 10 February 1998," The Hashemite Royal Court of Jordan, www.noor.gov.jo/main/iucnamm.htm.

"Petra, The Great Temple Excavation," www.brown.edu/Departments/Anthropology/Petra/excavations/history.html.

Michelle Piccvillo, "The Madaba Archeological Park and the Mosaic School at Madaba, Jordan—An Account of a Project," wysiwyg.//49/http://www.geocities.com/Athens/2888/Madaball.html.

"Tati's Art Gallery," www.axoxs.com/TAG_K.htm.

"Telecommunications in the Middle East," www.mideast law.com/telecommunications_in_the_middle.htm.

"USAID/Jordan: Strategic Objective (SO) Three: Improved Access to and Quality of Reproductive and Primary Health Care," www.usembassy-amman.org.jo/USAID/populate. htm.

Milton Viorst, "Jordan: A Moderate's Role," wysiwyg://22/ http://www.theatlantic.com/issues/81 mar/hussein.htm

WEBSITES

Arab Net (www.arab.net). Online resource for the Arab World in the Middle East and North Africa.

Arab World Online (www.awo.net). An information source with direct access to all aspects of the Arab world.

Mediterranean Free Trade Zone Environment Monitor (www.foeme.org.mftz). The MFTZ Environment Monitor is a monthly bulletin covering issues related to the Euro-Med Partnership/MFTZ preparations that are of environmental and social significance.

Welcome to the Jerash Festival Home Page (www.jerash festival.com.jo). Information about the annual cultural event.

The World Fact Book 1999 (www.odci.gov/cia/publications /factbook/index.html). The World Fact book is prepared by the Central Intelligence Agency for the use of U.S. government officials. It contains maps and facts about countries of the world.

INDEX

PICTURE CREDITS

ABOUT THE AUTHOR

Karen Wills has practiced law and taught writing courses at the college level, and is a freelance writer of fiction and non-fiction. Besides writing, she loves to hike and cross-country ski in Glacier National Park, near her home. She is an active advocate for the preservation of America's wilderness areas. She has a grown son and daughter. Her master's degree in English and her Juris Doctor are both from the University of North Dakota.